Developing Effective 16–19 Teaching Skills

Developing Effective 16–19 Teaching Skills aims to enhance the competence of trainee teachers in secondary schools and FE colleges as they confront 16–19 teaching for the first time. Based around the new standards set out in Qualifying to Teach and the FENTO standards, the book will help trainee teachers address the different teaching strategies needed to teach post-16 students.

Full of case studies and questions for reflection, this comprehensive textbook includes chapters on:

- Effective 16–19 teaching
- Avoiding preconceptions 16–19
- Planning for differentiation
- Subject expertise
- Assessment 16–19
- Active learning in the 16–19 classroom
- The importance of the tutor role in 16–19 teaching
- Learning with colleagues: developing a career in 16–19 teaching

The book is organised to prompt trainee teachers to draw more fully on 16–19 evidence and enhance their competence and confidence in teaching that phase. It also aims to support NQTs and inexperienced teachers in their quest to develop effective 16–19 teaching skills.

John Butcher is Staff Tutor in Education and a Senior Lecturer in the Centre for Research and Development in Teacher Education at the Open University.

Developing Effective 16–19 Teaching Skills

John Butcher

RoutledgeFalmer
Taylor & Francis Group

LONDON AND NEW YORK

First published 2005
by RoutledgeFalmer
2 Park Square, Milton Park, Abingdon, Oxon OX14 4RN

Simultaneously published in the USA and Canada
by Routledge
270 Madison Ave, New York, NY 10016

RoutledgeFalmer is an imprint of the Taylor & Francis Group

Typeset in Bembo and Myriad by
Keystroke, Jacaranda Lodge, Wolverhampton
Printed and bound in Great Britain by
TJ International Ltd, Padstow, Cornwall

British Library Cataloguing in Publication Data
A catalogue record for this book is available from the British Library

Library of Congress Cataloging in Publication Data
A catalog record for this book has been requested

ISBN 0–415–32837–3

This book is dedicated to my brother Paul,
the book he will never write.

Contents

Preface

The 16–19 phase of education is under closer scrutiny than ever before. Policy is volatile, with debates in England and Wales continuing to focus on arguments about the organisation of the 16–19 curriculum and whether standards of achievement are improving. However, the separate worlds of school sixth form and college teaching are inching closer together. Despite the fact that 16–19 teachers rarely have an opportunity to discuss teaching and learning with their colleagues, never mind those based in another institution, the most important work continues to be done by 16–19 teachers, with their students, in the classroom.

This book is intended to support trainee and inexperienced teachers as they develop 16–19 teaching skills. Having taught in comprehensive school sixth forms and FE colleges, and currently supporting the initial training and continuing professional development of teachers, my concern is with effective practice in the classroom. This book opens up the secret garden of 16–19 teaching, suggesting effective strategies, while recognising the current limitations of relevant training.

I welcome feedback on the ideas in this book. If your institution would like a workshop or a series of staff development sessions on effective 16–19 teaching, please email the author: j.s.butcher@open.ac.uk

Acknowledgements

I am indebted to my wife for her continuing support and to my children for their enthusiasm. The ideas in this book have developed over the years in numerous conversations with colleagues in the Centre for Research and Development in Teacher Education at the Open University, with PGCE students and their mentors, and with former teaching colleagues at Stantonbury Campus. I am especially grateful to Dr Hamilton Davies for his astute comments on draft chapters, and to the Open University for the three months study leave in which most of this book was written. Any errors, of course, are my own.

List of abbreviations

AEA	Advanced Extension Award (replaced former S level from 2002)
A level	General Certificate of Advanced Education, now consisting of AS and A2
AS	Advanced Subsidiary, usually taken in Year 12, carries value in its own right
A2	Second part of A level, usually taken in Year 13, not a discrete qualification
AVCE	Advanced Vocational Certificate of Education (formerly GNVQ Advanced)
FENTO	Further Education National Training Organisation
GCSE	General Certificate of Secondary Education (usually resits in 16–19)
GNVQ	General National Vocational Qualification (Intermediate and Foundation levels)
KS5	Key Stage 5, effectively the 16–19 phase
ITT	Initial Teacher Training (usually pre-service, graduate entry for secondary, often in-service for college teachers)
LSC	Learning Skills Council (regional agencies funding 16–19 education)
NQT	Newly Qualified Teacher
Ofsted	Office for Standards in Education (inspects 16–19 education in schools and colleges, and ITT)
PGCE	Postgraduate Certificate in Education
QTS	Qualified Teacher Status (awarded to trainee secondary teachers once they have met the Standards. Not transferable with an FE teaching qualification)
TTA	Teacher Training Agency (responsible for all routes into secondary teaching, but not college teaching)

1   Introduction

I really appreciated the opportunity to talk about 16–19 teaching and learning . . . we haven't had time to do that for years.
(Experienced 16–19 teacher evaluating a staff development session in school)

I certainly think a PGCE doesn't address how to teach A level.
(Mentor)

I have not come across any particular help with post-16 teaching and I would be glad of more guidance.
(Trainee secondary teacher)

WHY THIS BOOK?

This handbook is aimed at trainee secondary and college teachers, and existing school and college teachers, interested in enhancing their competence and improving their

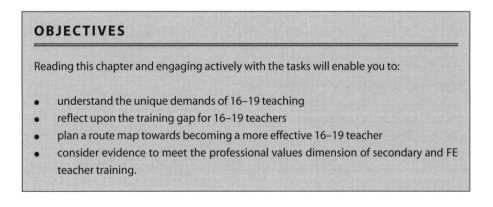

OBJECTIVES

Reading this chapter and engaging actively with the tasks will enable you to:

- understand the unique demands of 16–19 teaching
- reflect upon the training gap for 16–19 teachers
- plan a route map towards becoming a more effective 16–19 teacher
- consider evidence to meet the professional values dimension of secondary and FE teacher training.

confidence in teaching 16–19 students effectively. Drawing on primary and secondary research data, the book is meant for a professional audience with the intention of providing fresh insights into the skills needed to be an effective 16–19 teacher, and to stimulate thinking about effective practice in the classroom. It recognises the increasing convergence of the 14–19 curriculum across schools and FE and foreshadows any proposed link between current Standards for school teachers and those for FE teachers (Ofsted, 2003). In addition, it is hoped the book will encourage the academic and policy-making community into taking 16–19 teaching more seriously.

This book was written in recognition of the fact that 16–19 education continues to represent such a significant shift from compulsory secondary schooling in England, Wales and Northern Ireland. There are three distinct features to the phase:

- Different demands: most significantly for teachers, the curriculum and assessment systems on offer to 16–19 students are completely different from the National Curriculum 11–16, from SATs taken at 14 and from the group of GCSE assessments generally available at 16.
- Selective choice: the 16–19 student's school or college is likely to have selected them for a particular academic, vocational or pre-vocational pathway.
- Lack of homogeneity: unlike pupils in 11–16 secondary education, post-16 students (as they are likely to be called, although the Qualifying to Teach Standards call them all pupils) have chosen to remain in education on completion of the compulsory phase. Staying on in full-time education is the one shared feature common to all 16–19 students. Their abilities, motivations, attitudes, aspirations, institutional contexts and personal circumstances are so varied that they should not be viewed as a homogeneous group, although they are often (wrongly) represented in policy documents as such.

So the phase is unique, and implicitly, much of the literature endorses the powerful belief in a break in schooling at 16 as a crucial rite of passage. There are examples of challenge to this mindset, especially the work of Hodgson and Spours (1997, 2003) who advocate a change to a 14–19 phase to provide comprehensive continuity and cohesion across academic and vocational curricula. However, as Hodkinson (1998) recognises, a break at 16, though problematic, is an institutional and structural reality. So this book concentrates on the need for effective teaching 16–19, while recognising an emerging notion of a 14–19 curriculum.

Importantly, this book focuses on 16–19 rather than 16–18 in recognition of the increasing number of students who seek a one-year course or programme of study to enable them to progress to the most popular two-year A level or AVCE route. These students thus spend three years in tertiary study. Such flexibility accords with current policy targets which proclaim achievement by 19 as a benchmark of success, and with the legal status attached to full-time study up to 19.

So what is it that makes particular groups of 16–19 learners really distinctive from their younger peers? How much account can a teacher take of factors affecting individual student learning like: ability, motivation, personality, attitude, age, home life, previous learning experience and learning style? This question is important, because even highly prescribed courses like A level or AVCE (see Chapter 2) allow teachers, individually or in teams, to operate professionally, to judge and evaluate what they can do to facilitate effective learning. This can include decisions made about sequencing teaching opportunities, planning individual lessons, and organising resources which maximise opportunities for effective 16–19 learning.

There are undoubtedly an increasingly broad range of students electing to stay in full-time post-compulsory education, and as a consequence teachers would be wise to seek effectiveness in a diversity of approaches to teaching and learning 16–19. Ofsted recognises that these approaches are not the same as those found effective 11–16. For example, in English:

> A level represents a move into a specialist academic area from GCSE with its own methods of study and specialist terms.
>
> (Ofsted 2001g, p. 1)

If methods of study are different across other A level subjects (and the examples in this book will seek to demonstrate this), and the same is true in other 16–19 courses, there is a need for teachers to think very carefully about how they plan, teach and assess lessons. Very particular and focused teaching strategies are required throughout 16–19 education.

The jump from a secondary phase (currently 11–16 in most local education authorities) to a tertiary phase (16–19) has been present in slightly different forms for many decades. However, the changes introduced in Curriculum 2000 (QCA 1999, DfEE 2000) have had a major impact on the work of 16–19 teachers (see next chapter). The introduction of public examinations (Advanced Subsidiary) during or at the end of Year 12 has increased immensely the pressure on many teachers, who may feel themselves to be tied on a treadmill of 'delivering' heavy content in order to prepare students for assessment demands. This not only saps teacher morale, it can mitigate against exciting and creative approaches to teaching.

In addition, the design of the AS level has itself been questioned. The role of January and June modules, and a new retake culture, has shaken up what previously was a stable sequence of timings in the organisation of 16–19 assessment. There are fears that, as a result of such pressures, encouragement is given to a more didactic and superficial approach to teaching and learning. Teachers are under pressure to ensure coverage of the specifications in a short timescale (one academic year, September to the end of May) for young adults who were in Year 11 only a few months before. The effect of this can be to prioritise teacher-led input. At risk can be the opening up of student engagement in the learning process.

Clearly, not all 16–19 students are engaged in 'academic' A level work. But for the increasing number of students opting for a vocational alternative to A level, the academicising of the vocational curriculum to resemble A levels (Phillips and Pound 2003, p. 173, and see Ofsted 2004b) can affect teachers and their approach to teaching. This is important, and is a challenge to some of the assumptions that have previously underpinned BTEC National and Advanced GNVQ teaching. Such changes will be considered in some of the examples in the book.

Talking with 16–19 practitioners it is apparent that, as a result of changes introduced in Curriculum 2000, there is a shared concern that the assessment tail is wagging the curriculum dog even more than previously. If this is true, there can be little time for teachers to reflect upon the most effective teaching and learning strategies to meet student needs. As a consequence there may be even fewer opportunities for teachers to share good practice than there were in the past. The pressures of planning, the doubling of coursework requirements (and related standardisation), the need to facilitate end tests, all contribute to reduced time and opportunity to engage in 16–19 professional development.

In addition, an increasing focus on school and college improvement over the last decade has seen far more public attention on published results by the 16–19 cohort of a school or college (usually but not exclusively A level results) in the local and national media. This scrutiny is often intense and is fanned by the publication of league tables. It can also be amplified by the associated perception that Ofsted measures the effectiveness of 16–19 teaching by an over-reliance on the unmediated statistics of A level results, with too little account taken of the value added by 16–19 education. The key question emerging from this is whether 16–19 teachers, and those who evaluate them, really know the impact of effective teaching skills on such results?

It might also be argued that, in 16–19 education, too many generalised assumptions are made by policy makers about learner needs, despite the fact that 16–19 students do not form a hermetically sealed, distinctive and identifiable group. There are simply too many factors affecting the learning style of individual 16–19 year olds to propose any kind of one-size-fits-all model. Yet the importance of effective teaching in the 16–19 classroom continues to be ignored or undervalued by policy makers. For example, the significant changes proposed in the 14–19 Green Paper (DfES 2002) made little of the teaching skills required for such changes to be effective. Similarly, the developing arguments around the benefits of a shift to a Baccalaureate style qualification 14–19 or 16–19 (as initiated in Finegold *et al.* 1990, and considered afresh in Phillips and Pound 2003 and DfES 2004) pay little attention to potential teaching approaches when the bounded single subject is no longer king and the 16–19 student is no longer offered a series of discrete, assessment-driven packages.

To shed fresh light on 16–19 teaching, it is worth reflecting on the range of institutional contexts in which students and teachers might engage in 16–19 education. Individual school sixth forms have their own local history and are often used in marketing literature as a flagship indicator of a school's effectiveness. Such instances can include:

- references to A level grades achieved
- the proportion of post-16 pupils entering Higher Education
- the staying-on rate from pre-16
- aspects of school culture and ethos such as Head Boy/Girl, prefects, uniform/non-uniform
- the range of extra-curricular activities offered.

Most, but not all, local education authorities support systems which include schools with their own sixth forms. Of course not all sixth forms match the popular media stereotype of traditional A level examination factories. There may be sixth-form centres serving the needs of a cluster of schools organised on a collegiate basis. It is noteworthy that school sixth forms dominate in some subject entries, for example providing the bulk of A level entries in Geography, five times more than sixth-form or FE colleges.

However, in an increasing number of local education authorities there may be sixth-form colleges in lieu of, or even competing with, local school sixth forms. There may be Tertiary colleges in which academic and vocational courses are offered to post-16 pupils from a number of feeder schools. There may be FE or Technical colleges offering academic provision for full-time students amongst a plethora of vocational courses, often in competition with school sixth forms. Each may brand itself in relation to the distinctive achievements of its 16–19 students.

Tasks

Interspersed throughout each of the chapters in this book will be a series of tasks encouraging the reader to reflect upon a particular aspect of 16–19 teaching. The tasks are important for two reasons. First, because they provide a prompt to engage with the ideas raised (and are therefore intended to encourage a somewhat deeper consideration of 16–19 teaching). Second, given the limited opportunities for trainee teachers, newly qualified teachers and even experienced teachers to discuss aspects of 16–19 teaching, they provide an agenda for formal or informal meetings with colleagues in which 16–19 teaching can feature.

Task 1

Consider the context in which your 16–19 teaching takes place. Education is fraught with confusion over definitions: for the purpose of clarity, this book represents 16–19 teaching as being about academic and broad vocational teaching, which is likely to be located in school sixth forms or sixth-form colleges or the academic departments of FE colleges.

Is 16–19 a minor part of your teaching commitment in a big secondary school?
Is it a substantive role in a huge college, or a little part-time teaching in a small sixth-form centre or tiny department?
How will this professional context affect what you plan to do?
How will this impact on your behaviour in the 16–19 classroom?
How much support do you expect from colleagues in your 16–19 teaching?

Your responses to these questions will inform the amount of attention you can give, and the professional energy you can expend, in making your 16–19 teaching more effective. If most or all of your teaching is 16–19, engagement with the ideas in this book will be crucial to your professional development. If your involvement is limited, the ideas are equally valuable but may need to be accommodated alongside other priorities.

THE SECONDARY GAP: WHAT OF THE STANDARDS AND THE LITERATURE?

Unfortunately, school teachers and trainee secondary teachers interested in 16–19 teaching are ill-served by the plethora of generic secondary-school-based books on teaching skills. Most texts fail to distinguish the particular strategies needed for the unique demands of post-16 learners, implicitly assuming generic strategies can be applied across very different contexts, or ignoring 16–19 completely. Some take a subject focus (for example in English, Andrews 2001) but still largely ignore the particularity of the 16–19 dimension (a notable exception in Mathematics is Haggarty 2002). It is rare to find a whole book (Powell 1996) devoted to 16–19, in this case Geography.

This lack of discourse surrounding 16–19 teaching skills would matter less if initial training provided school teachers with clear confidence and competence in teaching 16–19 effectively. Theoretically, the best grounding for effective 16–19 teaching skills ought to be developed during initial training. For many teachers in secondary schools given 16–19 classes, and teachers in sixth-form colleges, this will be, or will have been an 11–18 Postgraduate Certificate in Education. The Standards for QTS (Qualified Teacher Status) make very specific requirements of post-16 teaching, so that those awarded QTS must demonstrate:

they are aware of the pathways for progression through the 14–19 phase . . . are familiar with Key Skills.

(TTA 2002, p. 7)

those qualifying to teach post-16 pupils teach their specialised subjects competently and independently.

(TTA 2002, p. 12)

Unfortunately, these are two statements buried amongst many more. The 16–19 phase, whether A level or vocational alternatives, is an aspect of 11–18 teacher training which is often neglected by trainers and schools (Butcher 1998, 2002). In addition, following Curriculum 2000, it is more and more difficult for trainees to gain experience in AS and A2 classes. It is also significant for those teachers with an interest in 16–19 teaching that QTS induction can be completed at a sixth-form college, but not at an FE college. It is thus intended that this book comprehensively address that dilemma and support the requirements for QTS (see 'How to use this book', pp. 14–16).

Increasingly in Initial Teacher Training, universities and other providers are considering re-designating or re-badging their secondary 11–18 PGCE courses as 11–16 to fully conform to the requirements of Qualifying to Teach (TTA 2002). This is not to criticise either training institutions or their partner schools for an inability to squeeze a quart into a pint pot (24 weeks of practical experience in a 36-week full-time postgraduate course). Rather it is a recognition of the dangers and difficulties faced by training institutions and their partner schools when Ofsted inspectors can award training institutions a non-compliance or 'technically' non-compliant grade if experience in and understanding of the 16–19 phase is not fully demonstrated. The impact of such a threat on an institution, on its staff and its reputation cannot be underestimated. Hence the real danger that 16–19 teaching, in schools in particular, will enter a vicious circle of inadequately covered initial training and marginalised continuing professional development. The result will be a significantly reduced number of teachers qualified to teach at A level. How then are 16–19 teaching standards to be maintained, or even improved?

The training system for 16–19 teachers based in schools is thus under pressure at the same time that QTS is awarded to secondary teachers for competence across two adjacent Key Stages. With the increasing emphasis on 14–19 as a coherent phase, this is beginning to focus some trainees' career aspirations on Key Stages 4 and 5. This book will seek to highlight rather than marginalise effective 16–19 teaching skills as part of that debate about 14–19 education. It will also support the trainee secondary and sixth-form college teacher by exploring the value of effective strategies in the 16–19 classroom. The material and associated tasks will simultaneously help them produce, as necessary, evidence to meet the Qualifying to Teach Standards.

Take as an example Standard 3 (Planning, expectations and targets). In working with a mentor to plan, teach and assess a sequence of History lessons in a topic on Weimar Germany in Year 12, evidence would count towards meeting the standards for QTS 11–18. For example:

3.1.1   Set challenging teaching and learning objectives which are relevant to all pupils in their classes [knowing] the pupils, evidence of their past and current achievement, expected standards for pupils of the relevant age range, range and content of work relevant to pupils in that age range.

3.1.2   Use teaching and learning objectives to plan lessons, and sequences of lessons, showing how they will assess pupils' learning . . . take account of and support pupils' varying needs so that girls and boys, from all ethnic groups, can make good progress.

(TTA 2002)

This example of planning a sequence of Year 12 lessons could certainly contribute to meeting the Standards. An ITT mentor could support a trainee's development by discussing the Year 12 group beforehand, and could comment on the trainee's planning in the light of the learners' capabilities and prior educational experiences. The mentor could link this to a post-observation discussion of how the planned learning objectives had been met. It would also provide an excellent exemplification of the range of teaching undertaken at first and subsequent job interviews.

Task 2

For qualified teachers: *how well did your training course prepare you for the demands of 16–19 teaching? With hindsight, what would you wish had been included, what do you wish your mentor had supported you in?*

For trainee teachers: *how much input have you had from your course on effective 16–19 teaching? How much access to 16–19 teaching have you been able to have during practice in school? What else would you have liked?*

Teaching at 16–19 is in an unenviable Catch-22 situation. For most secondary school teachers, access to 16–19 teaching is limited, and most have had little sustained input or experience during initial training. So developing effectiveness in the classroom is often dependent upon a pro-active approach from individual teachers.

THE FURTHER EDUCATION GAP

The current system of FE teacher training does not provide a satisfactory foundation of professional development for FE teachers at the start of their careers . . . few opportunities are provided for trainees to learn how to teach their specialist subjects, and there is a lack of systematic mentoring and support in the workplace.

... FENTO standards ... do not clearly define the standards required of new teachers.

(Ofsted 2003, p. 5)

The increasing literature on teaching in further education (e.g. Harkin *et al.* 2001, Fawbert 2003) is valuable for all trainee teachers interested in 16–19, but can be difficult to relate to teachers working in schools, despite evidence of the sectors inching towards one another through policies advocating increasing collaboration. This difficulty in transferring useful FE knowledge to 16–19 teachers in schools (and vice versa) is partly because the FENTO Standards (see start of following chapters) are not applicable to a school setting and partly because the emphasis in books aimed at FE tends to be on the demands of purely vocational teaching in college settings.

It is also significant that the generic tradition in post-compulsory (non-school, vocational) education is very different to that found in the subject domination of secondary school teacher training. Texts supporting new and intending teachers in FE (e.g. Armitage *et al.* 2003) are generic rather than subject-focused, to complement the generic courses provided to accredit training (City and Guilds, Post-compulsory Cert Ed., PGCE (FE)). FE has a strong tradition of teachers seeing vocational or subject expertise as more important than knowledge of teaching, as well as different subject traditions and cultures to schools. Thus teacher educators and teacher developers across the school and FE sectors find it difficult to have a dialogue with one another when the training Standards and contexts they work to are so radically different. This contributes to a regrettable marginalising of informed debate and dialogue about improving teaching and learning in the tertiary phase. For college teachers, training can be ad hoc, and subject mentor support is rare (Ofsted 2003).

Teachers in further education have also experienced a seismic shift in expectations about their professional role in recent years. Since September 2001 all unqualified FE teachers are required to hold, or work towards and achieve within a specified time, a recognised and appropriate teaching qualification. This is divided into three discrete stages, to meet the needs of a range of trainees in different delivery patterns. FE teachers on fractional appointments are expected to gain a Cert. Ed. or equivalent within a maximum of four years. Unqualified new part-time FE teachers are required, according to their role to achieve a Stage 1 teaching qualification (a minimum basic survival kit) within one year, and a Stage 2 qualification (the full range of skills needed to be effective) within two years. Full-time teachers, and those on fractional contracts, are required to meet Stage 3, which goes beyond teaching skills, embracing management and curriculum development. All FE teaching qualifications have to be based on FENTO Standards (see FENTO website www.Fento.org), which are wide ranging and more holistic than those used in school-based training (which reflect a more competence-based model).

The predominant model in FE is of on-the-job training aimed at new or inexperienced teachers (many of whom hold vocational qualifications rather than a degree). This in-service training can be thorough, but for the individuals concerned, this has to be fitted in with the challenging demands of paid unqualified teaching. On-the-job training can also present college management with short-term problems if teaching is found to be ineffective. So the opportunity to read and reflect upon good practice in teaching 16–19 year olds is important.

It is intended that a text which raises questions about the effectiveness of 16–19 teaching strategies will provide a valuable support to college teachers developing evidence to meet the FENTO Standards. FENTO Standards include seven broad headings (A – G) framed within a professional values dimension (Standard H). For example:

Standard B Planning and preparing teaching and learning programmes for groups and individuals
    B1 identify the required outcomes of the learning programme
    B2 identify appropriate teaching and learning techniques
    B3 enhance access to and participation in the learning programme

Standard C Developing and using a range of teaching and learning techniques
    C1 promote and encourage individual learning
    C2 facilitate learning in groups
    C3 facilitate learning through experience.

Standard D Managing the learning process
    D1 establish and maintain an effective learning environment
    D2 plan and structure learning activities
    D3 communicate effectively with learners
    D4 review the learning process with learners
    D5 select and develop resources to support learning
    D6 establish and maintain effective working relationships
    D7 contribute to the organisation's quality assurance system

Standard E Providing learners with support
    E1 induct learners into the organisation
    E2 provide effective learning support
    E3 ensure access to guidance opportunities for learners
    E4 provide personal support for learners

Standard F Assessing the outcomes of learning and learners' achievements
    F1 use appropriate assessment methods to measure learning achievement
    F2 make use of assessment information

These are then broken down again to between six and ten qualitative skills statements at the Certification level, which focus on how well work can be done on a continuum from novice to expert. FENTO emphasise that FE teacher training is not about 'can do' tick lists. So FE teachers can look to Chapter 4 in this book to support their development of evidence to meet FENTO Standard B, Chapter 6 for FENTO Standard F, Chapter 7 for FENTO Standard C and D, Chapter 8 for FENTO Standard E.

However, Ofsted noted:

> In contrast to ITT for secondary teachers, FE teacher training has received little recent independent scrutiny through inspection.
>
> (Ofsted 2003, p. 4)

And in the first report into FE teacher training, they highlighted failures in training which they compare unfavourably with training for secondary school teachers:

> In contrast with secondary school trainees, who have teaching experience in at least two schools, pre-service FE trainees have experience in only one college, and in-service trainees rarely gain first-hand experience outside their own workplace.
>
> (Ofsted 2003, p. 24)

> Unlike ITT for secondary teachers, most courses for FE teachers are not designed to provide subject or vocation-specific training. . . . assumed that trainees will already have the necessary specialist skills.
>
> (Ofsted 2003, p. 26)

> The variable nature and quality of work-based specialist mentoring contrast markedly with secondary ITT, where the role of the mentor is central . . . typically have dedicated weekly meetings with trainees.
>
> (Ofsted 2003, pp. 26–27)

Task 3

For the FE teacher: *how much support have you had from experienced colleagues in developing effective teaching skills?*

This is a crucial question, underlining the general absence of mentor support in the professional culture of FE teacher training and the consequent underplaying of subject support. If you work in FE, what sort of support would you think most appropriate?

These comparisons with secondary ITT are indicative of a significant policy shift which should lead to the most effective and established practices in school-based training (especially mentor support) becoming embedded in FE teacher training. Perhaps in the future, FENTO's focus on 16–19 teaching and learning will influence the QTS Standards.

THE DOMINANCE OF A LEVELS

It would be no surprise to suggest that the A level element of the 16–19 phase is the one most recognised by the general public. Not only has A level traditionally been perceived as attracting a higher status than vocational alternatives (witness entrance to the 'top' universities), but every August the A level is subject to close, sometimes hysterical media and political scrutiny when the outcomes of two or three years' teaching, in the form of GCE public examination results, are published. The headlines are predictable:

- Have standards fallen/risen?
- Have syllabuses and examinations been 'dumbed-down'?
- Have examinations been fairly and efficiently marked?

This annual debate between the hand-wringing harbingers of doom (interpreting improvements as evidence of lower standards) and the congratulators (assuming evidence of better teaching) is about achievement at the level of the total cohort rather than the individual. Such scrutiny usually stops at the door marked 'outcome', while the processes underpinning 16–19 education are rarely considered. Thus there is little explicit public interest in the quality of 16–19 teaching, despite the contribution effective teaching makes to those grades. Yet having enjoyed, or more usually endured fifteen minutes of fame, the A level element of 16–19 education retreats to its more usual position on the periphery of educational debates, emerging periodically in politicised discussion of curriculum policy and standards. Unfortunately, discussion of the effectiveness of 16–19 teaching disappears still further into the shadows.

So, as you seek to develop your 16–19 teaching skills, it is worth reflecting upon the values that underpin 16–19 education. When A level is seen to dominate as the 16–19 benchmark qualification, what are the outcomes that are expected 16–19? What control can teachers have over inputs like choice of topics, or hours of study? It is worth remembering, A levels are subjects examined by a Board, but the school or college (through their teaching staff) organise a programme of study, effectively an A level curriculum to be followed by each individual. It is in this way that individual 16–19 teachers have a genuine opportunity to impact on the effective learning of their students.

Task 4

For those considering, or already engaged in A level teaching, consider the following with a colleague:

To what extent is the A level curriculum highly prescriptive?
To what extent is the A level curriculum neutral?
Before your teaching begins, it is worth reflecting on the values you associate with A level, and the outcomes you expect for students. What are they?
How does the A level curriculum affect your subject? How do you pick your topics and for how long do you teach them?

Careful consideration of such issues will put you in a better position to make professional judgements. Your answers can then underpin effective teaching in 16–19 lessons.

PROFESSIONAL DEVELOPMENT NEEDS IN 16–19 EDUCATION

'Gaining more experience 16–19' is a phrase often mentioned in the induction targets for secondary NQTs (newly qualified teachers). This is because opportunities to gain enough experience and to have adequate support in 16–19 teaching are often missing during initial training. This is not to claim there is no 16–19 training, but that the experience of individual trainees in the 16–19 classroom can be partial and somewhat ad hoc. As a result, NQTs can be insecure and lack confidence in tackling 16–19 teaching with the same reflexivity and creativity accorded to 11–16 teaching. For many, there is a professed need to develop thinking about 16–19 issues, as well as a need to build on often extremely limited access to post-16 teaching (Butcher 2002, 2003a, 2003b). In busy schools there can be limited support for this, so this book seeks to address that shortfall. The chapters that follow provide a useful and concrete agenda for NQTs and their induction mentors (TTA 2003) in the learning journey to probation being signed off.

Even for longer-serving teachers, experience of teaching 16–19 can be patchy, with new developments in 14–19 curricula and the impact of Curriculum 2000 presenting significant targets for professional development. Whether used in the early professional development phase, or as part of a continual updating, this book can provide teachers with a valuable source of ideas and strategies. For some subjects in secondary schools with an established staff, 16–19 teaching can be viewed from outside as something of a closed shop. Even experienced teachers, presented with a first or rare opportunity to take responsibility for a post-16 class, will benefit from some confidence boosters and access to a repertoire of effective teaching strategies. This book supports that and also provides ideas for gathering evidence related to 16–19 teaching which will help meet the Threshold requirements for secondary school teachers.

For those seeking, or responsible for, career enhancement in the 16–19 phase, the book provides material to reflect upon and to develop an agenda for job and appraisal interviews which draw out important 16–19 teaching and learning issues. Examples would include leading and managing AS or A level moderation or internal verification on a GNVQ course.

Finally but importantly, as teachers increasingly look to develop themselves against professional standards which may or may not incorporate accredited in-service postgraduate qualifications, the book offers many ideas for small-scale research topics or action research projects in teaching and learning 16–19. Examples might include observation of post-16 student behaviour and the impact of gender imbalance, or teacher talk in 16–19 classroom discussions.

Task 5

Select one aspect of your 16–19 teaching that you would most like to improve (draw on the wording of the QTS or FENTO Standards if necessary). Discuss it with an experienced colleague. Can they observe you teaching in order to offer some constructive feedback on how to be more effective?

The key here is to make best use of a 16–19 teaching observation by an agreed focus which culminates in a manageable number of targets for future development. These should then be followed up in subsequent observations.

HOW TO USE THIS BOOK

The core of the book is devoted to practical ideas, some generic, some subject-focused, which aim to support 16–19 teachers in schools and colleges to improve teaching and learning in this exciting and exacting phase. In most chapters a case study is included to illustrate effective practice and illuminate issues for all 16–19 teachers. While often focusing on the work of Advanced level teachers at AS and A2, the book is not exclusively about A level teaching. Rather, it recognises and celebrates the increasing diversity of pupils found in this post-compulsory phase, from GCSE through GNVQ, AVCE and AEA. It argues that a model of post-16 teaching (and training) based on a traditional single-subject specialist A level teacher no longer suffices. It suggests there is much to learn from the particular skills and emphases of GCSE teachers in Key Stage

4, of pre-vocational and vocational 14–19 teachers in schools and (increasingly) colleges and of the best practice in some undergraduate education. For reasons of space and focus, it follows the remit of Ofsted in excluding the particular situation of teachers in work-based education and training, but it is the intention of the author that professionals in this so-called purely vocational area would be able to draw on and adapt many of the ideas explored here.

Chapters 3 to 9 each commence with a reminder of the relevant QTS and FENTO Standards. These are meant to prompt further reflection on how the ideas following can contribute evidence for trainee teachers to meet those Standards. For more experienced teachers, the Standards provide a reminder of what is considered a baseline of effective practice that can be prioritised in 16–19 teaching.

This is not necessarily a book to sit down with and read at one sitting. Having got this far, it is recommended tackling Chapter 2 which provides an overview of the complex context in which teachers in school sixth forms, post-16 centres, sixth-form colleges, tertiary colleges and colleges of further education currently work. Understanding this context is important to underpin effective teaching. We need to know why the 16–19 curriculum we are teaching is like it is, and how it is intended to meet the needs of a diversity of learners. Chapter 2 features an important reflective task based on an autobiographical case study which is intended to focus attention on the post-16 learner and their response to teaching.

The book then identifies, in Chapter 3, what researchers, inspectors and policy makers consider effective post-16 teaching strategies. A case study with associated tasks is based on effective 16–19 teaching in Science and Mathematics. This is intended to present a positive model of good practice and to exemplify a range of subject-specific and generic strategies proven to be outstandingly effective.

Chapter 4 investigates the critical differentiation needed to plan effectively for 16–19 teaching. It draws on the research highlighting the kind of misconceptions teachers have about 16–19 learners. A case study with associated tasks based on effective 16–19 teaching is included to support thinking about planning for 16–19 classes.

Chapter 5 illuminates the importance of a 16–19 teacher's subject expertise, and links that to effective assessment of learners. A case study and associated tasks based on research in English teaching 16–19 is included.

Chapter 6 looks at the significance of assessment in 16–19 education, connecting this to a case study and associated tasks based on the importance of feedback to illustrate some of the ideas.

Chapter 7 analyses the critical role of active learning and carefully thought out discussion in the 16–19 classroom. A case study and associated tasks based on the use of ICT is included, together with research on the gender imbalances found in many 16–19 classrooms.

Chapter 8 revisits the importance of the tutor role in 16–19 education, emphasising the crucial role in supporting independent learners generically. A case study and associated tasks based on supporting 16–19 SEN students is included.

Chapter 9 raises a number of issues in learning effectively with 16–19 colleagues and developing a career as a 16–19 teacher. An autobiographical case study and associated tasks is included.

Chapter 10 concludes the book by signposting a pathway for developing effective 16–19 teaching skills. An agenda for improved training, based on the needs of teachers in 16–19 classrooms, is featured.

Each chapter considers and exemplifies a broad range of strategies designed to support the most effective post-16 teaching. The examples and ideas explored in each chapter are intended to be stimulating, exciting and thought provoking, representing the best in post-16 teaching. Chapter 7 incorporates suggestions about the use of ICT in 16–19 teaching, something increasingly important but an element that can be neglected in teachers' initial training and subsequent professional development.

Task 6

It is worth completing this introductory chapter with a consideration of an important question:

How has 16–19 teaching suffered over the years in its attempts to straddle two very different traditions, the academic and vocational?

At its most extreme, this question can be represented on the one hand by the academic status of A levels and A level teaching, fostering an ideology which is completely dominated by the fiercely guarded primacy of the subject and subject departments. A levels are subjects and Awarding Bodies examine subjects. School and sixth-form college teachers are usually presented as being subject specialists rather than teachers of 16–19 year olds. Their training has been to demonstrate competence through their subject teaching. On the other hand, schools and colleges organise programmes of study to be followed by individual A level students. In FE, the other extreme of what is in fact a continuum sees the tradition of vocational course specialists working together in course teams as far stronger.

Such imagined oppositions between A level teachers and those working on vocational programmes prevent 16–19 teachers from talking to one another, learning from one another's ideas, even visiting one another's classrooms. This book aims to bridge that divide, to open up the 16–19 classroom, to synthesise effective practice in school sixth-form and college teaching for the benefit of all learners. It is hoped it will encourage all interested professionals to reflect on what they are doing in the diversity of the 16–19 classroom and why.

While picturing a class of 16–19 students pursuing full-time education, it should be remembered that many students in the 16–19 age range will be taking GCSE, A level or vocational qualifications on a part-time basis, at evening classes or through various day-release packages from employment or training schemes. While not emphasising their needs, it is intended that the ideas in this book are usable by the teacher of part-time students as well.

CONCLUDING REMARKS

The issues raised above are varied, interrelated and important to the 16–19 teacher. In summary, they include:

- limitations of initial training
- inadequate continuing professional development possibilities that are relevant to 16–19 teaching
- ongoing assumptions about 16–19 teaching based on the dominance of A levels
- pressure on 16–19 teachers to resort to a didactic (teacher-led) model to accommodate Curriculum 2000.

A combination of all four means there could be a real danger of merely reporting a deficit model of 16–19 teaching in a book like this, and attracting slightly weary nods of recognition from experienced colleagues at the inadequacies described. It is the intention to avoid that trap by highlighting and exemplifying what is known about the best, most innovative 16–19 teaching in all its diversity, while suggesting what to avoid and why.

Enjoy the read, reflect on the ideas and I hope you go on to develop the excitement, fun, creativity and liberation of really effective 16–19 teaching.

HEADLINES

Training for secondary teachers in 16–19 teaching can be considered inadequate because:

- QTS Standards underplay competence in 16–19 teaching.
- During placements, partner schools are often too stretched to prioritise 16–19 teaching.
- The academic literature is very thin on teaching 16–19 effectively.
- Training for FE teachers is not subject-specific, and is often in-service rather than pre-service.
- Curriculum 2000 assessment imperatives force A level teachers in particular to revert to teacher-directed approaches, regardless of their effectiveness.

2   16–19 education contextualised

There is a head of steam throughout the [16–19] system for change. It is true that there has been change but now people feel they need more.

(DfES 2004)

WHY IS CONTEXT IMPORTANT? HOW DID WE GET HERE?

Context is of critical importance because ongoing political issues continue to impinge on 16–19 teaching. In essence, these issues are about the need to broaden the post-16 curriculum, to improve access to post-16 education, and to introduce new skills without threatening standards.

AS, A2, AVCE, AEA, GNVQ, BTEC and GCSE provide a bewildering array of acronyms, something 16–19 education is particularly bedevilled with. Advanced Subsidiary, Advanced, Advanced Vocational Certificate of Education, Advanced Extension Awards, General National Vocational Qualifications, Business and Technician

---

OBJECTIVES

Reading this chapter and engaging actively with the tasks will enable you to:

- understand how the current 16–19 curriculum was arrived at
- reflect upon the academic/vocational divide 16–19
- take an informed view on what 16–19 education will look like in the future
- critique the Tomlinson recommendations.

Education Council and General Certificate of Secondary Education are the most popular, but by no means the only courses currently on offer in schools and colleges 16–19. For the trainee teacher, the newly qualified teacher, or the teacher new to 16–19, the range of courses can present a bewildering menu of new content, new assessment systems and most importantly, new teaching challenges.

The 16–19 curriculum that teachers encounter today (see QCA 1999, DfEE 2000) has emerged after a long period of heated debate (culminating in the Dearing Review, 1996) about the most appropriate curriculum for 16–19 year olds in the twenty-first century. During this debate, arguably lasting half a century and still smouldering, the status of the A level has been steadfastly preserved. This implies a very particular and focused set of teaching strategies in many 16–19 classrooms. Are teachers of A level, and its vocational alternatives, adequately prepared for this?

Reflecting on the preparation provided by Initial Teacher Training is important in order to contextualise these issues. Although some universities have traditionally offered a voluntary post-16 option, since the early 1990s trainee secondary school teachers on an 11–18 Postgraduate Certificate in Education course have all been required to produce appropriate evidence to demonstrate competency in the Standards right across the pupil age-range. This has meant that classroom practice and subject knowledge requirements have had to be met not just through work within the mandatory National Curriculum 11–16, but also the 16–18 (or increasingly the 16–19) curriculum. For many this has been limited to a perfunctory opportunity to experience teaching AS in Year 12.

With increasing public pressure on a school's A level results (not least from parents), partner schools have become understandably guarded about letting trainee teachers loose on sustained 16–19 teaching. This problem has been exacerbated by the introduction of AS and the modularity of the A level curriculum. So a new secondary teacher's experience in the 16–19 classroom, particularly in relation to Year 13, can be very limited.

Rather than approach A level teaching, or the myriad of other 16–19 teaching possibilities cold, and rather than attempt to understand such teaching in isolation, it makes far more sense for beginning or inexperienced 16–19 teachers to start with an understanding of why 16–19 education takes the form it does. A chapter on context in a book on effective teaching skills 16–19 is important because of perception. Perception is crucial, because the image of 16–19 teaching that trainee teachers, NQTs and inexperienced 16–19 teachers carry with them from their own experience of being a student in that phase can colour approaches taken and fix a mindset about 16–19 which presents problems when planning for effective 16–19 teaching.

CASE STUDY: IS THERE A STANDARD 16–19 LEARNER?

Contextualising the 16–19 learner is an important starting point. Reflect back for a few minutes on your own experience of being in 16–19 education. For some (like me, growing up in the 1970s) this will have meant 'staying on at school', joining the sixth form. So why does a 16 year old choose to remain in education? Why did I choose to stay on? Looking back 30 years, I am still unclear. It was not love of the academic life, infatuation with my subject or because I had enjoyed the years of compulsory education so much. Nor was I aiming at university.

Staying on just felt like a kind of natural progression having achieved seven very average O levels. I had no clear idea of what post-16 education entailed, of why I was there and what it would lead to. While such an autobiographical description seems quaint today, I wonder if the experience of many 16–19 learners is so different now?

I can recall little about the quality or effectiveness of the teaching. In English I remember that the opening piece of assessed work was being left on my own (was this independent study?) to research and write an extended essay on two authors of my choice who would still be studied in the future. It was admitted this was to 'burn-off' the dilettantes who regarded English as a soft option. I am sure I learned something but whatever it was did not come from good teaching. I also recall reams of photocopied notes in History with the emphasis completely on the content of the syllabus, and a week-long Geography field trip, the social impact of which overshadowed any of the content covered during the rest of the two years.

I recall little written feedback or explanations to help me improve my marks. I did not learn how to learn, because I was not taught how to learn. My expectations were so vague and unformed by any teacher target-setting that, on receiving my results, I felt nothing of the euphoria or disappointment seemingly experienced by post-16 students today.

Task 7

Reflect on your own experience of studying A levels or their equivalent. What can we expect the experience of a post-16 learner to be? What can we expect the expectations of students to be of their 16–19 teaching?

I would not wish to imply that all 16–19 learners will fit a similar pattern. Indeed, back in the 1970s a number of my friends chose to leave school at 16. A number of my other friends chose to continue their 16–19 education at the local college. All of them were keen to leave school, and none of them regretted it, although not all of the latter sustained their courses to completion and some moved quite quickly into work. So there were then, and continue to be, many and varied reasons for staying in full-time 16–19 education. It is important to consider your own reasons for continuing with your education. What were the pressures, what were the pulls in other directions, what were the alternatives?

HOW HAS 16–19 EDUCATION BEEN PERCEIVED?

It is only when we start to take responsibility for teaching in the 16–19 phase that our own experience of being a 16–19 learner informs our trial-and-error teaching. This early experience allows us to reflect upon and revise our understanding of factors such as student attitude and previous attainment. For some 16–19 teachers, relatively recent memories of successful undergraduate study will blend seamlessly and unproblematically into the 16–19 experience. For others, sixth form or college will seem a distant period of notetaking leading to terminal examinations. Neither perception is likely to open up adequate consideration of the range of current 16–19 learners' needs, nor to encourage teachers to engage fully with current 16–19 issues. This is ironic, since in secondary schools, 16–19 teaching is usually a highly esteemed part of a teacher's professional role, both through individual self-image and external measures of status. But there are inevitably other priorities during initial training and continuing professional development, and 16–19 might not receive the degree of attention it merits. Too often 16–19 teaching in schools can be perceived as a soft option, something that does not have to be planned for with the same care as Year 9 on a wet afternoon. This perception is exemplified in the difficulty of squeezing relevant aspects of 16–19 teacher preparation into overcrowded 11–18 PGCE courses.

There are a number of reasons for 16–19 teaching being considered a soft option. There can be a perception (in one's own initial expectation, or from other colleagues) of fewer discipline challenges than in 11–16 teaching. This, as Chapter 7 seeks to demonstrate, is not always true. There can be a notion that smaller class sizes will automatically make teaching easier. (Of course not all 16–19 classes are small, and as governments keep telling us in relation to such issues, size isn't everything.) There might be an expectation that pupils who choose to study a specific subject at advanced level will be as highly motivated as the most focused undergraduate. Consequently, an assumption can be made that subject knowledge requirements will be met with the kind of undifferentiated strategies misremembered as being successful at undergraduate level. Of course the problem faced by 16–19 students confronted with a teacher who really knows their stuff but cannot teach it (or else can only 'reach' the A-grade candidates) is not unknown. But it is not a situation to be condoned.

Even during secondary teachers' initial training, mentor prioritising of developing competence in Key Stage 3 and 4 to ensure trainee survival 11–16 can serve to marginalise the significance of learning to teach 16–19 effectively. As a consequence, planning for 16–19 teaching might be naïve, with little recognition of the contentious arena to be entered. The result can be ineffective teaching.

In practice, teachers new to 16–19 are more likely to experience something of a culture shock, not realising the political battleground the post-16 curriculum has become. A number of potential training issues emerge:

- Will trainees have had a chance to enter into debates about the relative merits of academic and vocational provision?
- Will trainees have spent time considering different approaches to 16–19 teaching?
- Have trainees considered the efficacy of content-driven lecture-style spoon-feeding of 'traditional' 16–19 teaching, in which the teacher retains control throughout?
- Have trainees explored opportunities for a discussion-based seminar approach often espoused 16–19, but less often practised?
- Have trainees evaluated opportunities to explore skills-based experiential project work giving the student considerable autonomy?

Perception of 16–19 teaching is especially important since, in the thinking of many stakeholders, A levels continue to dominate the 16–19 curriculum in schools and sixth-form colleges. This mindset affects thinking about how to teach effectively in the 16–19 classroom. It also underplays the gap between expectations of students taking GCSE at 16, AS at 17 and then A2 at 18 or 19. This can have a profound impact on the experience teachers have in the 16–19 phase, and raises significant issues for the adequacy of the training and support those teachers have received: so why has 16–19 education taken the form it has?

A BRIEF HISTORY OF 16–19 EDUCATION: A LEVELS (UN)REFORMED

It can be argued that school-based 16–19 education in England, Wales and Northern Ireland operated, for fifty years until 2000, with a jealously guarded and relatively unchanging core (A levels) and changing fashions at the margins (various ongoing attempts to broaden or vocationalise the curriculum). Colleges have changed more, but the non-vocational curriculum offered in sixth-form colleges, tertiary colleges and the general academic departments of FE has stayed pretty much the same. A historian has described the school sixth form, even well into the second half of the twentieth century, as:

> . . . indissolubly linked with the ideals of the public and grammar schools . . . with a concept of [tertiary] education as being limited to a minority.
>
> (Judge 1984, p. 114)

This reminder about the implicit selection and labelling that went on (and arguably continues to go on) in many school sixth forms, raises important questions of college provision 16–19 too. Despite what is often a more open discourse of access, do twenty-first-century institutions providing 16–19 education continue to select and label students? What is your experience with 16–19 students in your institution?

Commentators (see for example Chitty 1991, Lawton 1992) have argued that 16–19 education has been a contentious, ideologically driven battleground since the introduction of the A level examination in 1951. Evidence supporting this assertion can be found in the regular (failed) attempts to broaden study in the school sixth form and related college provision, despite the fact that the 16–19 student population increased considerably over this period.

The history of aborted attempts to modify the structure of the A level provides a fascinating insight into why 16–19 teaching has often been taken for granted. Three years after the introduction of this single-subject examination to replace the old Higher School Certificate (which had been organised on a subject group basis), the Early Leaving Report criticised the wastage of talent, a view echoed by the Crowther Report of 1959 which saw specialisation as a constriction rather than a liberation. Over-specialisation and a lack of breadth were also highlighted in the Agreement to Broaden the Curriculum in 1961, but good intentions were sidelined by university demands for higher grades at A level. Other examples include three separate Schools Council proposals for reform:

- 1966: two major subjects, two minor subjects and General Studies.
- 1969: two-stage structure of five Q (Qualifying subjects) in what is now Year 12 and three F (Further) subjects in what is now Year 13.
- 1973: mix of N (Normal) and F (Further level) to be taken at the end of Year 13.

All were rejected, partly out of a fear of three successive years of public examinations, and partly out of university fears that lower standards would necessitate longer degree courses. What is of course absorbing about these abandoned ideas is the similarity to the thinking behind the 16–19 curriculum as introduced in 2000.

TVEI (Technical and Vocational Education Initiative) provided funding to develop interesting new models of teaching and learning 14–18 from 1983. This impacted briefly on 16–19 but the 1988 Education Reform Act effectively killed off this radical national project. DES proposals for Advanced Supplementary level qualifications were initiated in 1984 and introduced into schools and colleges in 1987. They attempted to broaden and complement specialist study by advocating a two A level + two AS model, with the AS examined at the same standard as a standard A level but with half the content and study time. However, the original AS was only ever optional, and signals from the university sector were at best ambivalent, so most schools and students chose to stick with a traditional three A level programme. Some of those students who did take AS found it impossible to reach the requisite intellectual level.

The 1988 Higginson report advocated a five-subject mix of AS and leaner A levels, but this was rejected by the then government's proclaimed intention of preserving the specialised 'gold standard'. Subject cores (SCAA, 1994) were an attempt to impose greater centralised commonality and coherence on the A/AS relationship.

So, despite flurries of activity, for fifty years it can be demonstrated that all attempts to move away from the 'three A levels or nothing' approach failed to garner sufficient support from policy makers and education professionals. Supporters of A levels dug into a tamper-free, essentially conservative position. Despite the alleged parity between academic and vocational pathways in the 1990s, Core Skills were embedded in GNVQ but not in A levels. This is evidence that vocational alternatives like GNVQ (because of their inherent interdisciplinary structure and overt skills development) were offering students more explicit outcomes than A levels.

Task 8

In discussion with a colleague in your department, consider why A level has stayed relatively unchanged for so long. What does the future hold for A level? Will that be a good or bad thing for your subject and your 16–19 teaching?

Despite Curriculum 2000, one thorny problem still bedevilling 16–19 education is the mismatch between an entitlement curriculum 11–16 (assessed by a range of GCSEs) and the specialist demands of A level studies between 16 and 19. According to Lawton (1992), the 1988 Education Reform Act left a policy vacuum by failing to tackle education and training 16–19. Of critical importance, as Whitbread argued (1991), were the implications for A level study following the introduction of a common examination at 16 (GCSE). This view is echoed by Harland (1991), Richardson (1993) and Kershaw (1994), all of whom analyse the missed opportunity to reform 16–19 education and to bring teaching methods more into line with the pre-16 educational experience.

The kind of breadth taught and assessed at 16 through the GCSE has always been in tension with academic specialism post-16. The GCSE was never designed to prepare students for the demands of studying A levels, but to offer an entitlement to almost all Key Stage 4 pupils.

So, the role of a hermetically sealed A level curriculum could be considered restrictive by:

- offering no linkages to vocational alternatives
- having no perceived relevance other than as a preparation for Higher Education

- allowing (even encouraging) pupils to discontinue whole subject areas like Science
- providing nil value to those pupils who only spent a year in sixth form
- offering nothing to show for those pupils (originally a quarter) who attempted them and failed to pass.

In view of successive governments' commitment to what has been presented to the rest of the world as a 'gold standard' in education, the A level remained until 2000 sacrosanct. It was politically and pedagogically separate from the rest of secondary schooling and from vocational training courses for the 16–19 age group. The impact of the Dearing review (1996) is important here. Constrained to maintain the academic rigour of A levels by a government in thrall to a very particular notion of academic excellence, an opportunity to broaden the post-16 curriculum was lost. Pound (1998) characterises the Dearing review as a conservative reform, which confirmed A level as the indisputable test of fitness for entry to Higher Education, in spite of the radically altered characteristics and changed context of 16–19 education over the previous forty years. However, the review ignored how such courses were to be taught effectively.

Responses to Dearing (Hodgson and Spours 1997, Stanton and Richardson 1997) continued the focus on policy and curriculum frameworks rather than pedagogy, with only the latter including some recognition of the diverse needs of post-16 pupils. Thus effective teaching strategies 16–19 continue to be off the radar of policy makers and academics. And yet, it is the engagement of teachers with the new curriculum structures, the teachers' abilities to motivate and develop student learning through carefully selected strategies, that will make 16–19 reforms work (or not).

Criticisms of A level as being over-specialised have been oft-repeated. Such concerns bear further consideration. The Schools Examination and Assessment Council described A level as:

> A narrow academic orientation . . . overburdened with content . . . and an inadequate range of assessment methods.
>
> (quoted in Richardson 1993, p. 2)

The root cause underpinning such assertions is that, in its original design, A level was conceptualised as a preparation for Higher Education. This is now problematic for two very significant reasons. First, Higher Education itself has changed enormously over the last fifty years. The United Kingdom has moved significantly towards a mass system of Higher Education rather than an elite system, with increasing numbers of 18–19 year olds and mature students embarking on degree-level study. This has been met with consequent shifts in expectations of students and the kind of curriculum and teaching which will best meet their needs.

Second, changing employment patterns and training opportunities have also had the effect of inflating expectations of education beyond the age of 16. The UK has had thirty years since the school leaving age was raised to 16 with an expectation that more and more students will gain the requisite five grade Cs or above at GCSE to qualify for entry to A level study in many sixth forms and colleges. As a result, increasing numbers of 16–19 students are choosing to continue in full-time education. Does specialisation meet the needs of all those who take A levels?

Such issues are important for the 16–19 teacher, because of the failure and withdrawal rates among sixth formers studying A levels (National Commission on Education 1995). Historically it has been noted:

> Many sixth formers then were following courses designed in principle for those going on to university, but were nonetheless completing their full-time education at the age of eighteen.
>
> (Judge 1984, p. 117)

In other words, a continuing emphasis on A level as a specialised preparation for three-year degree study should no longer be (if it ever was) an unthinking article of faith for 16–19 teachers. In such circumstances, what can suffer is the effectiveness of teaching. When syllabuses are recognised as content-heavy and assessment regimes dominate, how do 16–19 teachers get to develop stimulating teaching strategies aimed at a broader range of students?

It is also noteworthy that the Education Reform Act contributed nothing to the 16 year olds who left compulsory schooling with limited access to further education and training, and that fewer UK school pupils enjoyed advanced level education in comparison to our international competitors. While such observations fall outside the scope of this book, they provide an interesting backdrop to the hidden 16–19 curriculum.

Such issues gain importance given that the 1990s were marked by a policy rhetoric of parity of esteem between academic and vocational routeways, yet Canning (1999) asserts that the more academically qualified will be favoured over the vocationally qualified, and Eggleston (2000) claims that Year 11 tutors, as gatekeepers to post-16 education, connive with school systems which seek to select who stays on and what they are offered, reflecting class and ethnic bias. These are aspects of a veiled issue in 16–19 education which should form part of initial training or continuing professional development of 16–19 teachers. The impact of a skewed playing field for 16–19 year olds should inform the approach to planning and differentiation in the 16–19 classroom. This should form an important agenda item for discussion between trainee teacher and mentor, and as part of an induction target which features 16–19 teaching.

Traditionally, the emphasis on A level assessment was the terminal exam, for which grades A–E could be awarded, with N denoting a narrow failure and grade U unclassified. Following the introduction of GCSE, there was an increase in A level coursework to diversify academic assessment, but this was curtailed following the Code of Practice (SCAA 1994b) which imposed general subject cores in an attempt to promote equality and consistency across the Awarding Bodies (who of course depend for income on examination fees from schools), and to help HE and employers understand what had been studied and assessed. Up until the mid-1990s, A levels were taught and assessed in a linear fashion, with a spurt towards synoptic assessment of specialist knowledge at the very end of the two years.

Following this, modularisation was the major pre-Curriculum 2000 reform. This attempted to increase pupil motivation and introduce greater flexibility by shorter term goals and the facility to bank modules through discrete units or modules. These could be assessed (originally) at up to three points during the academic year. Synoptic assessment was included to test the understanding of connections between elements. With modularity, A levels required two years of hard work, with advanced level standards to be demonstrated during Year 12 as well as at the end of Year 13. Preparation for either teaching demand is not easy.

An example drawn from one A level subject (Geography) illustrates the attempt by some educators to transform A level itself from within at the micro-level of the subject. The sense of inertia represented by a long-standing highly theoretical A level syllabus can then be seen to represent the macro-problem of 16–19 education. Naish (1996) reminds us that in Geography, a subject that had been revolutionised in the early 1960s by the impact of quantitative data coming from the universities, pressures to change were building from the 1970s. Turton (1996) claims that the old A level pushed teachers to cover a large volume of syllabus content in a short period of time, thus forcing reliance upon didactic methods. Pressure to change was partly recognition of the limited connection between the separate branches of the subject, partly a broadening of Geography's educational aims into areas like conceptual learning and skills development, and partly the impact of new humanistic and behavioural perspectives from the universities. At A level, assessment was through essays in which regurgitation was highly valued.

Changes deriving from the Schools Council Geography 16–19 Curriculum Development project took a people–environment approach led by enquiry, decision making, and students managing their own coursework. Although the move to modularity produced a common core to Geography syllabuses (interaction between people and their environment, chosen physical environment, chosen human environment, personal investigation), it reduced the coursework to 20%. But significantly, the shift had come, and Geography was established as an enquiry-based subject 16–19.

During the 1990s, policymakers proclaimed the need for a choice of 16–19 qualifications to suit individual needs and talents. The driving force was an economic imperative: that Britain needed a better qualified workforce in order to compete in the market place against countries with far greater participation rates in post-compulsory education. Yet a contemporary analyst, as long ago as the 1970s, described the major issue in relation to post-16 education:

> The fundamental sixth form problem is of breadth versus depth. . . . A common comprehensive curriculum will have arrived by 2001.
>
> (Holt 1978, pp. 149, 147)

The latter irony notwithstanding, issues of breadth versus depth surrounding 16–19 education have been consistently raised in the literature. The orthodoxy of 16–19 education, represented by a commitment to retain A levels at all costs, has become historical baggage, arguably hindering progress. The key debates continue to be around the nature of the 16–19 curriculum itself. Particularly fierce is the opposition between proponents of early specialisation and depth of study (as exemplified by the two-year single-subject A level), and the proponents of breadth in the curriculum (as exemplified in the ideas surrounding post-16 Baccalaureate and the kind of interdisciplinary connections made on vocationally oriented courses).

Task 9

Look carefully at the A level specifications in your subject. Would you describe them as offering depth or breadth of study? Compare with what students are required to do on vocationally oriented courses. Is there a clear difference?

Although the relatively minor structural reforms instigated by Curriculum 2000 left A levels inviolate, the status quo had been challenged, not least by Key Skills.

VOCATIONAL ALTERNATIVES

The Dearing Review (1996) stymied, at least temporarily, any drift towards a comprehensive curriculum for 16–19 year olds. The report's recommendation was to adhere to three separate pathways (academic, general vocational and pure vocational), more clearly signposted but still discrete from one another. This was hardly radical, but perhaps the quiet revolution of Dearing was to initiate the possibility of opening up the Key Stage 4 National Curriculum with vocational opportunities via Part 1 GNVQ (a slimmer version of GNVQ equivalent to two GCSEs and aimed at 14–16 year olds). This could be seen as an important marker in the debate about vocational and pre-vocational work in schools (which has a significant history of its own). It has also enabled the idea of academic and vocational streams from 14 to emerge in government thinking.

The context for this is important. With the raising of the school leaving age in the 1970s, and the growing impact of youth unemployment in the 1980s, many comprehensive schools wanted to offer a broader and more accessible curriculum for the so-called 'new sixth' than an unsatisfactory programme of resits. However, the increasing co-existence of post-16 academic courses and vocational programmes (like CPVE, BTEC First or National Diploma, GNVQ at Foundation, Intermediate and Advanced) in secondary schools during the 1990s is one virtually untouched in the literature, although it was claimed:

> Significant numbers of comprehensive and upper schools across the country are building on a tradition of previous involvement with vocational awarding bodies . . . this has resulted in enthusiastic take-up of GNVQ.
>
> (Butcher 1998, p. 569)

Developments like the Certificate of Extended Education (CEE) were a short-lived attempt by the Awarding Bodies to provide for the non-academic sixth former, but when the 1979 proposals of the Keohane committee to offer a broad common core were rejected, the DES went for a more radical solution: the provision of vocational education in schools through the broad-based, integrated Certificate of Pre-Vocational Education (CPVE), available from the mid 1980s. Within a decade this had been killed off, to be replaced as part of NCVQ's remit to simplify the jungle of vocational courses with General National Vocational Qualifications (GNVQ). Interestingly for the school context, these were not a prescribed course but a set of outcomes, expressed as units of assessment, based on occupationally specific NVQs. They were designed to develop the knowledge, skills and understanding needed for work in broad occupational areas. Schools themselves had to devise a GNVQ course with minimal guidance on what teachers should teach. For one-year pupils, Foundation (NVQ level 1 equivalent to GCSE grades D–F) or Intermediate (NVQ level 2 equivalent to GCSE A–C) could be offered. GNVQ has been marked by ongoing tinkering since its inception.

The general lack of interest in non-A level 16–19 provision in the academic literature on schools may be explained by the continuing doubt as to whether vocational courses are proper activities for school sixth forms, even though it has been established that many comprehensive schools were waiting for real alternatives to A level for their 16 year olds (Sharp 1997). Some of the pedagogical and structural issues related to this are covered in research publications on the FE sector, but they generally ignore what was developing in secondary schools. The resultant danger is that secondary Initial Teacher Training is left promulgating a single-subject A level model of teaching post-16, which is an outdated and increasingly irrelevant one for today's schools and colleges. The issues raised in preparing trainee teachers and supporting qualified but inexperienced teachers adequately for effective teaching across the breadth of courses on offer post-16 are one rationale for this book.

None of this vocationalising of the curriculum, as the Dearing Review confirmed, threatened the hegenomy of A levels as the flagship 16–19 qualification. The primary alignment with the traditional academic curriculum 16–19 was between Advanced

GNVQ and A level. Both were to be studied full-time over two years, with each GNVQ unit notionally equivalent to one sixth of an A level. In theory 16 year olds could be offered a twin track curriculum, within a rhetoric of equality. A vocational course in school would in theory be identical to the GNVQ offered in the neighbouring college, although FE teachers in particular tend to have far more experience of delivering vocational qualifications. Because of the subject specialisms and narrow vocational experience of many secondary school teachers, a relatively limited number of vocational alternatives were available in most schools. For reasons you might wish to discuss, few selective or independent schools have been interested in broadening their 16–19 curriculum in a vocational direction.

It was in theory possible for pupils to 'mix and match' GNVQs with other qualifications, but in reality secondary schools pushed the able, highly motivated, fast-learning, higher achieving pupils towards those A levels which traditional universities valued, while less academically successful pupils, the slower learners, late developers and the less motivated were encouraged to stay on (bringing the school valuable 'on roll' income) to take GNVQs. Although the Dearing Report rejected proposals like the British Baccalaureate (see below), such thinking may have informed the committee's proposals to facilitate more coherent progression routes. However, until 2000 it was impossible to perceive 16–19 education as organised through anything like a comprehensive curriculum structure.

> ### Task 10
>
> *If you work in a secondary school, what are the arguments for suggesting that your vocational students would be taught more effectively in college?*
> *If you work in a college, what are your views on the increase in vocational teaching to 14–16 year olds?*

BACCALAUREATES AS THE ALTERNATIVE?

Externally, the main attempt to broaden an academic curriculum post-16 came from the International Baccalaureate (IB), first presented in 1971 as an international pre-university entry qualification operating in three languages: English, Spanish and French. Pupils continue to take six subjects, three or four at the higher level in two languages, a science, mathematics and one of the humanities, together with an option. The IB is offered in some UK schools, and numbers are increasing slowly, particularly but not exclusively in the independent sector. The IB continues to attract interest, but it has made a limited impact, in part due to its fearsomely academic reputation. It does not embrace vocational possibilities.

A British Baccalaureate was originally proposed as long ago as 1990 by the Institute of Public Policy Research (IPPR). Radically at the time, IPPR demanded an all encompassing British Baccalaureate to halt the academic/vocational divide. This was a modular, single, across-the-ability-range replacement for both academic and vocational pathways. It was based on the premise that at the heart of the post-16 problem was the academic/vocational divide. Critics of the existing twin track had noted that barriers between A levels and vocationally oriented programmes ensured hermetically sealed and inflexible systems. In the 1990s this amplified the concern over separating out pupils, educated comprehensively, into twin streams (academic and vocational) post-16. The adherence to a system of separate pathways post-16 was challenged from a series of positions. Payne (1991), drawing on a practitioner perspective engaged with curricular innovation post-16, criticised the system as it had developed in schools as being dominated by the status accorded to single-subject specialist A levels. Pressure to integrate academic and vocational routeways came from a variety of sources, with concerns continuing to centre on the need for relevant skills development and parity of esteem between the vocational curriculum and the historically more prestigious academic curriculum.

The British Baccalaureate envisaged all post-16 pupils mixing academic and vocational modules in a common framework. Kershaw (1994) challenged the twin tracks as inequitable, but criticised the British Baccalaureate proposal as impractical. Such debate may have contributed to the eventual modification of post-16 structures in Curriculum 2000.

Nor is the issue of 16–19 Baccalaureates settled. The Welsh Assembly has supported the piloting of a Welsh Baccalaureate (developed by the Institute of Welsh Affairs) in 11 colleges and 8 schools which gives equal weight to vocational and academic subjects balanced according to individual need, and which is accessible (they argue) to 80% of the population. Their criticism of Curriculum 2000 is that the rhetoric and aspirations of central government are out of balance with the actual provision of AS, Key Skills and vocational education in most schools.

CURRICULUM 2000

From September 2000 the results of the two-year QCA consultation on changes to A level, AS and GNVQ Advanced were implemented, instigating the most significant reform of 16–19 education for half a century. The original rationale for the review had been to broaden A levels and upgrade vocational qualifications, underpinning them (as was constantly reiterated) with rigorous standards and Key Skills. This was based on a belated recognition that the traditional 16–19 curriculum was too narrow and inflexible for the modern world, when the UK's European competitors in particular tended to offer broader but more demanding programmes of study including high-status vocational elements. The process of consultation highlighted specific concerns:

- the need for learners to improve their adaptability and keep career options open
- the need for greater flexibility to allow the combining of different types of qualifications according to different interests and needs
- the need to promote genuine parity of esteem between different types of programmes through an underpinning quality standards framework.

The press release at the launch (QCA 1998) included testimonials from key figures in the curriculum authorities, assessment authorities and employers:

This is an important step in ensuring that post–16 qualifications are ones which will meet future needs of students, colleges, HE and employers. . . . students will have more flexibility to combine academic and vocational qualifications in a way that hitherto has not been possible.

The recommendations take forward the unification of academic and vocational qualifications . . . a new flexibility, which will enable students to study in greater breadth. We are committed to high standards.

The development of opportunities for the inclusion of key skills into A levels, as a stand alone qualification, and the wider key skills are all moves which employers would like to see happen.

Critically, while acknowledging suggestions for incorporating aspects of 14–19 curriculum discussions or adult learning into the reform, the announcement of a national qualifications framework focused solely on the advanced qualifications for 16–19 year olds. The new framework was designed to:

- retain specialism where necessary for progression
- ensure coherence of provision without unnecessary duplication
- promote confidence in the relevance, consistency and intelligibility of all accredited awards.

The overarching goal was to maximise participation, achievement and progression and meet the needs of both HE and employers who were seeking students who had studied a broader range of subjects and gained a wider range of skills at advanced level.

In Year 12, a student on an 'academic' pathway is expected to take four, or (less usually) three or five subjects to Advanced Subsidiary (AS) level. The AS is a reformulated three-unit qualification representing the first half of the full A level. It is designed to encourage greater take-up of subjects, to provide more effective progression from GCSE into advanced level study, and to reduce numbers dropping out with nothing to show for their efforts. Awarded on an A–E grading, the AS counts as a qualification in its own right. Opportunities to develop and assess key skills are identified within the syllabus. Post-Curriculum 2000, a unitised system sets AS at a lower level than A level (but more demanding than GCSE) and generally allows one-third coursework. However, universities are still unclear about whether to count AS grades in offers, so schools and colleges have been forced to develop their own guidance on the benefits or otherwise of their students cashing in their AS qualifications early.

Task 11

Consider your subject in relation to the impact of AS in Year 12. Are teachers able to develop really effective teaching methods which engage all their 16–19 learners, or are they forced to lead from the front to get through the module specifications?

If you agreed that assessment pressures on students at the end of Year 12 constrain the kind of diverse teaching approaches possible in your subject, what can you do about that as a classroom teacher?

In Year 13 such a student is likely to continue studying three of these subjects to A2 in order to complete the full A level award. (The A2 does not currently make up a qualification in its own right.) The three English Awarding Bodies (a reduction to reduce the previous proliferation of specifications (formerly syllabuses) and allegedly maintain standards) are:

- Edexcel (formerly London and BTEC)
- OCR (formerly Oxford, Cambridge and RSA)
- AQA (formerly NEAB, SEG, AEB and City and Guilds)

Together with WJEC for Wales and CCEA for Northern Ireland, they provide specifications made up of six equally sized units (compare to GNVQ) with a choice of linear or modular assessment in each. Synoptic assessment, in which understanding of the whole syllabus is tested, is mandatory. Coursework is generally limited to a ceiling of 30 per cent in order (it is argued) to enhance the validity of overall assessment without compromising on rigour. Pass grades of A–E parallel the former A level grading system.

A student embarking on a vocational route will take an AVCE (a revised and renamed version of GNVQ Advanced). The full twelve-unit double award is equivalent to two A levels and is usually available in subjects explicitly related to the world of work such as Health and Social Care, or Business. It is awarded on an A–E scale like A level, so a successful student on a double award will receive grade AA down to EE. The six-unit version (effectively a vocational A level) consists of three compulsory and three optional modules and can be combined with standard A levels for pupils wishing to pursue both vocational and academic options. Some three-unit awards, equivalent to AS qualifications are also available. Assessment on AVCEs comprises approximately two-thirds a portfolio of skills relevant to a broad employment area, but units taken in Year 12 are assessed at advanced level. Arguably there has been a shift to more 'academic' teaching as the courses have been brought closer in design to A levels.

Advanced Extension Awards (AEAs) are newly designed 'world class' tests in thirteen major A level subjects aimed at the most able, but designed to be more accessible than the former S levels they replaced. They were available from 2002 and are intended to stretch the brightest A level students and allow them to demonstrate their understanding in greater depth. One intention is to illuminate for university admissions tutors any difference between the increasing number of A level entries predicted and achieving A grade.

Teachers at 16–19 would benefit from a hard look at how their teaching already develops Key Skills (or might do so in the future). Key Skills have been around in vocational qualifications (albeit in different guises as Core Skills and Common Skills) for many years. The first three 'hard' Key Skills (Communication, Information Technology and Application of Number) have been integrated into AVCEs but are separately certificated (de-coupled, assessed by short tests and a portfolio). Application of Number, like previously in GNVQ, has proved the most problematic.

The Key Skills qualification draws out evidence from students' programmes of study and is graded at level 1–4. The wider 'soft' Key Skills (Working with Others, Improving own Learning and Problem Solving) are reported on through an internally assessed portfolio, the progress file. However, unlike colleges, schools have not been funded to introduce Key Skills. They were merely signposted in the specifications. It would not be particularly bold to suggest that any successful implementation needs a whole-school or college approach, which will need to be linked to an unambiguous UCAS points score and an explicit connection to notions of employability. Consistency has not been fully applied, and until this happens, universities are unlikely to fully endorse Key Skills.

So Key Skills have not been a resounding success. Across 16–19 institutions, students endlessly debate their value. Where Key Skills workshops are offered, some attend, but not all take the examination. Well-organised students can achieve them relatively easily, but this does nothing to enhance their value or their reputation in the eyes of students. And many 16–19 teachers resist and resent the imposition of Key Skills on top of other significant changes (and increases) in their workload. As you develop your 16–19 teaching, it is vital to investigate how Key Skills are organised and supported in your institution.

Concern at the level of Maths learning seen in GNVQ, and worries that repeating a GCSE Maths is a less than useful experience for many students, has led to the

introduction of FSMUs (Free-Standing Maths Units) at levels 1–3 (Foundation, Intermediate and Advanced). These are equivalent to one-third of an AS level, and can
contribute evidence towards a Key Skills qualification. They allow a student an in-depth
development of a particular branch of Maths (for example, managing money at
Foundation or using and applying statistics at Advanced). Assessed through a portfolio
and a terminal examination, the work can be applied to a vocational situation. FSMUs
raise an important question: how can 16–19 teachers draw creatively on the knowledge
of students in their vocational specialisms?

Such developments raise significant dilemmas for 16–19 institutions. Should stand-
alone lessons be offered, or drop-in facilities, or should they be taught by non-specialists
during vocational teaching? Rather, teachers will need to draw on the knowledge and
examples of students in their vocational situation. But, if FSMUs are offered, there are
likely to be resource issues.

IS 16–19 SETTLED?

There continues to be much media debate about the possibility of a Baccalaureate-style
award replacing the post-Curriculum 2000 reformed A level, particularly fuelled by
the adverse publicity surrounding the 2002 exam-marking fiasco. The key issue is
whether to replace A levels or build on them. The AS appears especially vulnerable,
but policymakers are anxious to avoid the stresses on students, teachers and 16–19
institutions resulting from the recent incremental and piecemeal reforms. The logical
position would be for a more holistic approach to the 14–19 phase, with a coherent
14–19 programme for pupils, improved assessment procedures across the phase,
including examiners appointed in advance, and a unified framework of qualifications.
Given that Curriculum 2000 was intended to encourage greater breadth of subject
coverage 16–19, early research suggests that the four-AS model in Year 12 has failed
to increase breadth for individual students, thus intensifying the debate about the place
of A levels.

Problems to address include:

- lack of coherence (how do A level subjects relate to one another, how are they
  interdependent?)
- barriers to inclusion (how do students transfer between academic and
  vocational pathways?)
- progression: a series of assessment hurdles 14–19 means there are more snakes
  than ladders in the system.

Four policy initiatives at the start of the twenty-first century have continued the
piecemeal approach to reform reported above. Arguably, 16–19 teachers are still having
to read the runes to guess if major reforms are on their way. The 2001 White Paper

A levels have proved their resilience, but do they remain true to their original function of selection and exclusion despite the changes? Is A level still the jewel in the post-16 crown? Is A level only retained to maintain academic standards for 3-year UK university degrees, regardless of learner needs?

'Schools – achieving success' opened up a genuine possibility of a 14–19 curriculum embracing a mixture of academic and vocational pathways. This could place students on different pathways from age 14 and hence impact on teaching approaches.

'Success for all' (DfES 2002a) reformed the macro-management of the entire post-16 sector, mainly affecting FE and bringing it in line with the Learning Skills Councils. In so doing, school sixth forms were, for the first time, separated in one aspect of management from the rest of compulsory schooling. This placed school sixth forms in an interesting position, contributing to managed local post-16 initiatives with other providers (including colleges) and linked to LSC funding, yet still staffed by teachers often responsible for 11–16 teaching for the majority of their timetables. It does offer some potential unity to 16–19 education, and the possibility of some joined-up thinking in this area.

The Green Paper: 14–19 Education (DfES 2002b) proposed a loosening of the Key Stage 4 curriculum, with greater flexibility in 14–19 school/FE links. Proposals building on all these were formulated via the working group on 14–19 reform, chaired by Mike Tomlinson, which explored how to unify the qualifications framework through coherent learning programmes and changes in assessment systems. The publication of the consultative interim report (DfES 2004) heralded a lot of publicity and comment. Yet in none of these proposals is effective 16–19 teaching the priority.

Clarity about the purpose of comprehensive 16–19 education and the needs of diverse student groups have been highlighted in the recent policy developments affecting 16–19 education. A user-friendly pathway through a proliferation of 16–19 qualifications has been a long time in arriving and there remains debate over whether Curriculum 2000 has got us there. Effective teaching, rather than politicised curriculum interference, remains the most important contribution to a stable and stimulating learning environment for 16–19 year olds.

HEADLINES

- 16–19 learners are not, and never have been, 'standard'.
- 16–19 teaching is perceived by some as a soft option. It is not if done properly.
- Half a century of efforts at reform have left A level relatively unscathed.
- 16–19 vocational alternatives have struggled to escape a perception of being lower status.
- Curriculum 2000 has caused more problems than it answered. Is a Baccalaureate now needed?
- The Tomlinson Review ignores the role of the teacher and the need for effective teaching.

3 Effectiveness defined

Qualifying to Teach Standards

1.1   High expectations of all pupils . . . committed to raising their educational achievement.

1.2   Treat pupils consistently, with respect and consideration, are concerned for their development as learners.

1.3   Demonstrate and promote the positive values, attitudes and behaviours that they expect from their pupils.

3.3.1   They have high expectations of pupils and build successful learning relationships, centred on teaching and learning. They establish a purposeful learning environment where diversity is valued and where pupils feel secure and confident.

3.3.7   They organise and manage teaching and learning time appropriately.

3.3.8   They organise and manage the physical teaching space, tools, materials, texts and other resources safely and effectively with the help of support staff where appropriate.

3.3.14   They recognise and respond effectively to equal opportunities issues as they arise in the classroom, including by challenging stereotyped views, bullying or harassment, following relevant policies and procedures.

OBJECTIVES

Reading this chapter and engaging actively with the tasks will enable you to:

- reflect on the appropriateness of Hay McBer's model of teacher effectiveness
- compare Hay McBer with Ofsted's views on effective 16–19 teaching
- develop your own views of effectiveness in the 16–19 phase
- implement teaching strategies which will produce evidence to meet QTS Standards 1.1, 1.2, 1.3, 3.3.1, 3.3.7, 3.3.8, 3.3.14 and FENTO Standards D1–D7.

FENTO Standards

D   *Managing the learning process*

    D1   *establish and maintain an effective learning environment*

    D2   *plan and structure learning activities*

    D3   *communicate effectively with learners*

    D4   *review the learning process with learners*

    D5   *select and develop resources to support learning*

    D6   *establish and maintain effective working relationships*

    D7   *contribute to the organisation's quality assurance system*

WHAT IS OUTSTANDING 16–19 TEACHING?

This chapter aims to bring together best practice in 16–19 teaching from both generic approaches and subject-specific strategies. It presents a positive model in which the principle that 16–19 students should be encouraged to be exploratory, critical learners rather than passive recipients of teaching is central. The chapter also illuminates how effective 16–19 teaching can provide evidence to meet secondary ITT 'Qualifying to teach' Standards when working with a mentor or other colleague, and FENTO Standards for those training in FE.

What are 16–19 teachers aiming for? The challenges faced in the 16–19 classroom are distinctive from those faced in the 11–16 phase, or indeed the adult education setting. Indeed, describing 16–19 teaching in theoretical terms can be problematic, because it is a phase with learners (students) for whom the traditional notion of pedagogy (teaching children) is no longer entirely appropriate. To a considerable (and growing) extent, 16–19 education is equated to testing students in terms of a formal body of knowledge (AS, A level or AVCE). But the notion of an exclusively didactic 16–19 teaching style is one this book is attempting to moderate. Clearly, as the evidence in this book suggests, 16–19 students are not yet ready to be entirely self-directed learners. Theories drawn from adult education may not be any more helpful. However, andragogy (Knowles 1984), a theory of adult learning in which self-directed learners transform themselves into mature adults, is worthy of further consideration.

This theory of adult learning (though partly discredited in terms of the relevance of some of the claims made for it) places emphasis on the negotiated learning process. Adult learners are considered to be self-directed, with unique learning goals and a reservoir of experience on which to draw. This may be something policymakers might prescribe for students at the end of Year 13, in order to prepare them for the more independent learning required in Higher Education. But it does not describe the learning skills of the majority of 18/19 year olds, and universities regularly bemoan the limited study skills possessed by school and college leavers.

So a notion of a battle between pedagogy and andragogy in 16–19 teaching is too simplistic. There is a bridge for teachers to make between Year 11 and Year 12, but that is not the end of the story. Learners will find themselves on a continuum during this tertiary phase of their education. It is a phase needing continuing teacher support, but the nature of that support shifts over time according to individual needs. Understanding the internal differences and diversities between individual 16–19 learners is more important for effective teaching than worrying about whether pedagogy or andragogy is appropriate. Perhaps a new word is needed to describe 16–19 teaching.

We might expect students who have had a continuous experience of education from the age of 5 to be familiar with the expectations and routines of effective learning once they enter 16–19 education. But Year 12 teachers need to put aside preconceptions (often misconceptions) of what successful learners their students might already be. The goal of effective education in this 16–19 phase is that students will become more self-directed, independent learners, within a framework provided by examination board requirements and assessment regimes. Teachers have a crucial role in motivating their students to achieve that and the facilitative strategies teachers employ will need to channel the motivations that students have for remaining in full-time education. Crucially, how do teachers build on 16–19 students' previous learning experiences?

Challenges like this go some way to addressing the question: what is meant by becoming an effective (or more effective) 16–19 teacher? Education is ill-served by the range of taken-for-granted assumptions about teaching and learning in this phase. When assumptions about the primacy of content and assessment remain unexplored, stale re-runs of what teaching used to be like for passive learners are a real danger. This danger is exacerbated when 16–19 students are anxious about the time available before assessments, and hence pressure teachers to provide notes which they believe will 'substitute' for learning.

For too many years, any discourse about effectiveness in the 16–19 classroom has been muted, with little time or motivation for teachers in this phase to reflect upon the match between their own strategies and learner needs. As a consequence, some 16–19 teaching has remained locked in the amber glow of a golden age of teacher-directed, didactic teaching in selective A level classes. In the school sector, until recently, the inspection regime has tended to underplay the significance and impact of effective teaching and learning in sixth forms. Individual school Ofsted inspection reports have integrated limited evidence from 16–19 teaching within general comments which have prioritised evidence from 11–16 classrooms. Colleges have enjoyed a different inspection framework until recently.

Lately, Ofsted has taken a more pro-active approach in 16–19, publishing a series of post-16 reports on a subject-by-subject basis (Ofsted 2001a–r, 2002a–b). These have distilled evidence of good practice in individual subjects for both inspectors and senior staff in schools and colleges but have perhaps not been disseminated as widely as they might. Of course there are drawbacks with such reports in that some of the observations are based on small samples and are not always applicable elsewhere, especially if the context is not known. There is also an all-encompassing agenda about driving up standards which is not always made transparent, given the wider range of AS candidates now being taught. While I do not intend to present an Ofsted framework as the one route to effective teaching, the reports do provide an interesting prompt for consideration of effective 16–19 teaching on a subject-by-subject basis. They certainly provide a long-needed overview of what goes on in 16–19 classrooms.

This subject-specific focus will be combined with generic findings from the Hay McBer (2000) Model of Teacher Effectiveness report on effective teaching, and make connections with other observations. Hay McBer, a consultancy group, were asked by the DfES in 2000 to investigate and report on effective teaching skills. This chapter will seek to create synergy between the two perspectives, and articulate a clear case for what effective 16–19 teaching is.

WHAT DID HAY McBER SAY ABOUT EFFECTIVENESS?

It is worth framing a consideration of teacher effectiveness in the 16–19 classroom in the context of what Hay McBer concluded. The following nine points are a useful starting point (some of the language has been changed to reflect the 16–19 context):

- Clarity: *are students clear about the aims, objectives and context of each lesson?* For 16–19, as in most teaching, learners need to be absolutely unambiguous about what teachers want them to do, to know, to understand, and how this fits with what they have learned before and what they will be assessed on in the future. This raises the question as to whether 16–19 teachers can offer clarity even when they setting an exploratory task. Without that, learning (if there is any) will be directionless and ad hoc.
- Environment: *is the setting for the teaching comfortable and well-organised?* Some 16–19 teaching takes place in superbly appointed specialist rooms. Other 16–19 teaching (especially but not exclusively in schools) tends to be squeezed into whatever rooms or spaces are available when everything else in the institution is accommodated. The former is obviously the ideal. The latter may be reality for some, particularly new teachers given an hour or two of 16–19 teaching. If the latter is the case, it is critical to make every possible effort (with the assistance of your 16–19 students as appropriate) to shift furniture, move tables, ensure all can see the board or screen, and to ensure that you can circulate as necessary, in order to enable appropriate interaction and to facilitate discussion.
- Fairness: *is there justice and equality in the classroom?* This of course is imperative in the 16–19 classroom as in any other. Students, especially at the start of Year 12, may feel very differently about the new experience of choosing to stay in education. Some will rise quickly to the challenge, using their maturity and

confidence to good effect, relishing the opportunities that 16–19 education offers them. Others will feel very diffident. They may have come from other schools, from institutions with very different cultures. They may not have been especially successful in compulsory schooling. Students may have learning difficulties (often undiagnosed) or be learning English as a second or third language. Teachers must treat all with respect and do all they can to maximise appropriate opportunities for progression for all. Where there are open access policies, initial guidance is of crucial importance.

- Interest: *is there an appropriate level of stimulation to prompt student interest?* This is critical in 16–19 education, which still carries a reputation for an over-reliance on teacher-directed strategies. How much of any lesson or series of lessons taught to 16–19 students allows students to take charge of their own learning, to work in pairs or groups on a challenging task, to engage in peer or self assessment, to plan a schedule for a project, to role play or simulate and evaluate an activity rather than be told it by a teacher? How much are audio, video, outside speaker or ICT resources used creatively? There may of course be different opportunities across different subjects, but enthusiastic stimulation of student interest may share some generic approaches.

- Order: *are structure, organisation and discipline present?* To what extent has a 16–19 teacher organised activities to ensure students are engaged participants in a focused learning activity, in which teacher control and direction are present but hidden? Students cannot be left to their own devices too early. A clear framework for each lesson, planned and executed, will give learners confidence. This is especially true given the broader range of learners entering full-time post-compulsory education.

- Participation: *how far do students feel they can question and offer opinions in class?* This is crucial if active learning is to genuinely occur in the 16–19 classroom. Students need to gain self-assurance in exploring their own ideas, in questioning their peers and their teacher, in working together to solve problems. Without authentic participation, learners will be passive, and learning will remain at a surface level. This encompasses the notion that 16–19 students need to be helped by their teachers to become effective learners by meaningful engagement with intellectual capital.

- Safety: *are students safe from emotional and physical bullying?* Some students new to Year 12 may have been bullied or victimised in their previous experience of schooling. They may find it difficult to socialise with their peers in a new environment. They may feel isolated, lonely and vulnerable. It is thus important that the 16–19 teacher manages the learning with sensitivity, and offers all students equal opportunity to learn in a supportive environment. It is also critical that unacceptable behaviour between students is dealt with appropriately, and that parameters are explicit. Teachers need to feel supported in their own departments and institutions in this. It may be that schools have a better (although certainly not blameless) reputation in this area. How far is this idea of safety supported in your institution?

- Standards: *do students understand what is expected from them, are they encouraged to improve?* Target setting on a regular basis is important for 16–19 year olds. The pressure on results, whether in A level or AVCE courses, is intense, given their importance in relation to university entrance. The assessment hurdles arrive thick and fast in Year 12 and Year 13, and students deserve to be as prepared as possible for progressing. This places a vital responsibility on teachers to explain marking criteria, to justify gradings and to signpost where improvements could be made. If preparation has been thorough, expectations have been clear and targets have been explicit (and monitored) it should be exceptionally unusual for a student to receive a really disappointing grade for AS or A2. There is of course a tension in 16–19 education, with the pressure on examination sittings cutting across the ambition to use creative teaching and learning strategies.

- Support: *are students encouraged to try new things and learn from their mistakes?* This is tough when 16–19 seems to be dominated by the pressure of assessment objectives and league tables, but 16–19 students are embarking on a great educational adventure. They are free of the domination of the National Curriculum. They are mostly studying the subjects or courses they want to. They are entering a freer, more independent phase of their lives. If they can't explore new learning opportunities, in a context which provides both support and challenge, when can they? It is important to build opportunities into 16–19 teaching to enable students to dare to fail. It is just as important to ensure a framework is there for students to evaluate what went wrong and what can be learned from it.

Task 13

Think carefully about these points in relation to your own 16–19 teaching, or your observations of the 16–19 teaching of others. Do you easily achieve them all with little effort? Are there some that present particular challenges for the 16–19 teacher? Have you asked your 16–19 students about them: where would they see evidence of effectiveness or room for improvement in your teaching? Is there one suggestion that provides an appropriate agenda for a peer or mentor observation of your 16–19 teaching?

Such a checklist has its uses in starting the process of general reflection about our own teaching, but does not take us very far in the more fine-grained, deeper understanding of what we can do to develop effective 16–19 teaching skills. So what does Ofsted say that might take us a little further?

WHAT DOES OFSTED SAY ABOUT EFFECTIVENESS?

The key headline seems to be for 16–19 teachers to focus on what students need to learn, rather than what has to be taught. In A level Maths (Ofsted 2001k) this can be done by:

- Sound lesson planning, in which the sequence and progression of activities is structured, but with sufficient flexibility to meet individual needs.
- Time management, ensuring a fast pace, with an opportunity to check that learning objectives have been met.
- Good questioning skills, offering a high degree of challenge.
- Clear, staged expositions to model the mathematical thinking that students need to learn.

It is important to avoid the superficiality of teacher input followed by practice, with no opportunity for discussion of methods or ideas. It is also worth aiming at development rather than practice (which merely consolidates the same point over and over) or giving students no opportunity to engage with different ways of solving problems.

In Maths A level students need to become confident and accurate in their use of technical language. They also need to appreciate the links between different elements of the A level course in order to understand how a mathematical idea can be applied in an unfamiliar situation. A 16–19 teacher needs to organise the sequence of topics for coherence, continuity and progression. To do this it must be more than merely a 'learnt' technique, and teachers might want to check that student X is not simply following what student Y does when engaged in a co-operative task.

Effectiveness for the 16–19 A level Maths teacher thus depends on three factors within a context of appropriate, plentiful and stimulating resources, and the flexibility to challenge students:

- Subject knowledge: this has to be secure, and the teacher should enjoy presenting it enthusiastically. Appropriate subject knowledge can be exemplified by the teacher who understands and pre-empts student problems in the more demanding aspects of any given topic. It also links to a facility to group important ideas together for students to grasp.
- Expectations: while encouraging students to take increasing responsibility for their own learning (particularly the development of their own thinking skills), teachers need to balance the giving of information with the setting of

challenging work which will enable the acquisition of new knowledge. It is crucial they provide appropriate individual attention to weaker students, and that their whole-class questioning draws out where help is needed.

- Planning and organisation: build on previous learning by a constant routine of checking and refining student understanding. Careful questioning can establish whether students are following explanations.

A danger has been voiced by French (2002) that modular and unitised A level courses lead 16–19 Maths teachers back to a didactic, compartmentalised style of teaching and learning. This can be caricatured as: teacher presents topic; students work through examples individually as exercises; teacher dictates notes. This would appear to focus teacher thinking solely on the next 16–19 assessment hurdle at the expense of promoting a broader interest in the subject. How can such teaching stimulate and extend interest? How can the development of independent work be facilitated with such spoon-feeding? Where is the place for an intrinsic interest in Maths or the opportunity to link advanced study in Maths to the wider world? Such issues are not unique to Maths. How far is it true in your subject?

What is missing is the chance to discuss mathematical ideas, to explore blind alleys and false starts and to experience being stuck (and having to solve that problem). This could be particularly invidious if (as is alleged) too much investigation work at GCSE is accepted uncritically. How do students learn to construct and present mathematical argument (proof) using the correct language?

This can be compared to effectiveness in 16–19 Science teaching, in which:

> The best science teaching gives due attention to subject content, but additionally engages and motivates pupils to pursue scientific thinking.
>
> (Ofsted 2001p, p. 11)

Although unfortunately, it is reported that:

> Work in science subjects is often characterised by copious notes.
>
> (Ofsted 2001p, p. 16)

If giving notes, are science teachers simply getting students to copy them out, or are they compiled after discussion and guidance? Taking what emerge as three key headings across all reports, effectiveness in 16–19 Science teaching is characterised as:

- Subject knowledge: depends on mastery of the subject for A level and knowledge of relevant applications in industry for AVCE. This subject knowledge needs to be demonstrated with enthusiasm in order to stimulate student curiosity. This is exemplified by careful, clear explanations and answering questions correctly in order to prevent the misconceptions which can arise. Teachers can simplify complex scientific ideas through illustration. Effective teachers can also capture student interest by showing the relevance of topics studied by relating them through the use of models and analogies and topical material from the media. But they must be transparent about the limitations of such approaches.

- Expectations: effective teachers should insist upon appropriate terminology. They should ask challenging questions (pitched to individual students to challenge appropriately) which press beyond one-word answers. Superficial questioning never gets under the skin of scientific concepts. Imprecision in student responses should be gently corrected.

- Planning and organisation: provide opportunities to apply knowledge to solve unfamiliar problems. Teachers should have the confidence to use demonstration if it is likely to be more effective in aiding learning than student practicals. Planning and evaluation should be encouraged if a practical is used, but should be integrated with theory. There should be a clear and explicit sense of what should be learned in practical sessions.

So good, assured subject knowledge is about passion for the subject, in which the teacher should be an expert. Effective teaching depends upon the energetic, animated use to which subject knowledge is put, including the ability to explain clearly to students who are not yet expert. Ofsted (2001a) refers to science 'subject character' by which is meant good subject knowledge applied in a motivational way. It is worth considering what this means in relation to your own subject.

Task 14

Reflect on the relationship between your own subject knowledge and what you are required to teach 16–19. Are you secure in that? Do you have 'subject character'? Have you seen 16–19 teachers who have?

Expectations include the challenging strategies and skills by which these are addressed. Planning covers the well-structured provision of appropriately inclusive learning opportunities with questions asked at the right time. All three seem crucial to effective 16–19 teaching. Yet these might not quite mean the same thing across different subject disciplines.

For example, in 16–19 Design and Technology, subject knowledge is explicitly linked with teachers having a clear vision of the twin rationales for the subject: to stimulate imagination, creativity and innovation; and to develop a product to meet precise specifications (Ofsted 2001e). This is then demonstrated in high quality teacher demonstration of skills, the careful use of subject-specific language and frequent references to industrial/commercial practice. Teacher interventions, it is claimed, should not inhibit creativity.

In the same subject, high expectations are described as being about attention to detail (and safety!) alongside a culture in which students are expected to work hard, to persevere and to innovate. In the most effective work reported on, this mature attitude to work is inculcated rigorously by teachers in Year 12 and often supported by email contact outside lessons. Teachers of 16–19 Design and Technology need to be particularly aware of the improvement that students can make over time, recognising that the best work explores and creates anew by analysing in depth, and that only then can risks be taken.

While a range of different teaching methods should be expected (class, tutorial, seminar, interview, and open learning are mentioned), teachers should be aware of an over-heavy reliance on the teacher when students are working with CAD/CAM systems. This raises important questions about teacher and student use of ICT in the 16–19 classroom. How can it be utilised to enhance effective learning? How can it be used to release students from reliance on their teacher? The use of ICT by the 16–19 teacher is taken up in Chapter 7, but it should be noted that complex issues are raised about the context in which 16–19 teachers work, and the resources available to them.

Another important question is how students learn when units are taught by different teachers. Who is responsible for making the links and connections for students? One partial solution, as described in Constable (1999) is to commence each new intake into Year 12 with a task integrating all design specialisms (for example, A level Art, Design, Food, Graphics, Photography, Textiles and GNVQ Art and Design). The intention in such an approach is to:

- offer students a holistic view of design
- integrate the convergent thinking of problem solving with the divergent thinking of creativity, irrespective of the discipline
- team build (both teachers and students) by sharing goals and tasks
- introduce a 'wow' factor after GCSE by opening up the excitement of the real world and the possibilities of higher education
- use ICT for research and to produce powerpoint presentations
- celebrate with a public event displaying named work, promoted to local companies, parents, universities and PGCE students.

Immersion is critical here. Teachers have excited students at the outset, have provided ongoing feedback and have facilitated a public celebration which boosts confidence. Crucially, the work done meets A level and GNVQ criteria. It is also reported as providing the opportunity for an in-house 'corporate identity' to be introduced for all 16–19 assignments and tests. This is something to be encouraged across all subjects, so students have a more secure sense of continuity across teachers and as a course unfolds.

Another issue in Design and Technology is that in AS and A2, ideas for design briefs should ideally come from real-life contexts, and from organisations that will provide A level students with feedback on how their idea developed. There is always a difficulty in making such a client appear genuine rather than bolt-on. A good example of how to use external resources to facilitate this can be found in Capewell and Norman (2003) who draw on the work of a source outside the school and local environment (in this case a funded 'sustainability in design' project) to frame authentic tasks.

Subjects in the Arts, requiring creative responses as well as 'academic' ones, attract similar, but rather particular attention from Ofsted in relation to effective 16–19 teaching. Music teachers (Ofsted 2001n) are commended if a secure command of subject knowledge is in place, together with a varied repertoire of strategies and a sensitivity to pace. As well as employing clear explanation, the 16–19 music teacher should be confident about demonstrating a particular musical technique to improve student skills. They should encourage performance and composition of the highest musical quality, partly by penetrative questioning and partly by encouraging students to evaluate their own work. Interestingly, ICT use is praised when used for more complex techniques such as composition.

The A level, AVCE or National Diploma music class, Ofsted argues, should have an air of focused study and creative response. The atmosphere should be one in which students feel they can be critically supportive of one another's efforts. Students should be encouraged to work things out for themselves, the teacher should stand back from making too many precise suggestions about, for example, compositions. Discussion needs to feature musical vocabulary, and application across different musical forms. Theory needs to be consolidated practically, and professional contextualisation is important, particularly but not exclusively in vocational music courses.

Resources to support this ambition are especially significant in the Arts, and vital in effective 16–19 music teaching. Are practice rooms available outside timetabled lessons? Does equipment at least resemble professional practice? This can be compared to 16–19 Dance teaching, in which the provision of designated studios with mirrors and changing facilities is considered important (Ofsted 2002a), or Drama and Theatre Studies (Ofsted 2001f) which requires a designated space to accommodate performers and audience with blackout, lighting and sound systems.

In any subject, the choice of first topic for Year 12 students is crucial: teachers will want to present something challenging but manageable. They have to decide whether to approach afresh something covered previously in GCSE (building student confidence by drawing on something 'known'), or to galvanise students with something brand new (this is exciting, but students are going to have to move up a gear. Is there support in the teaching for this?) Whichever gambit is chosen, the content, teaching approach and assessment should link or bridge the gap between GCSE and AS level.

The key strategy at 16–19 is to transfer the responsibility for learning gradually from teacher to student. This can be supported by an open approach to questioning, followed by a sensitive approach to involving those students who did not initially volunteer.

Variation in teacher-led and student-centred activities is important, with a recognition that in a context of increasing class size in popular 16–19 subjects, of pressure to reduce contact time and seemingly reduced funding, it is very important to think about what students can do, and are prepared to do, in their own time. Examples might include writing up class notes, making notes from text books and viewing video material. It is worth considering, in a discussion with a colleague, what else might be appropriate activities for students to do in their own time.

Former views can of course change. Ofsted (2001a and 2001h) has acknowledged that Geography 16–19 is not primarily about the acquisition of information. Rather, effective teachers guide and encourage students to develop the skills of analysis and critical argument and to get under the skin of real and often controversial issues by exploiting their topicality. There is a recognition that visual resources (but not more than five years old!) bring Geography to life, and that teachers draw on extensive data and resources to teach students to assimilate, to prioritise, to synthesise and to edit. On the one hand, students need to understand how physical features are formed, on the other they have to be able to plan for decision making. Thus the tension in the 16–19 Geography classroom is between an over-reliance on teacher input versus independent learning. It is also about secondary sources versus primary sources (the fieldwork) and the recognition that students can often offer only tentative or incomplete inferences. How then can teachers develop a distinctive geographical voice for their students?

Good practice comes from the teacher's knowledge and enthusiasm, related to expectations of accurate definitions from students. It is linked to carefully set work with clear expectations and errors corrected, and good examples of how to do fieldwork. Teaching strategies will include role play and simulations utilising a wide range of resources to stimulate understanding. It is also considered imperative for teachers to ascertain a student's previous knowledge of a topic, in order to consider implications for teaching.

The kind of investigative work which has to be undertaken by Geography students in Year 13 for A2 is a good example of the kind of preparation teachers have to put in during Year 12. A range of practical techniques and skills have to be developed before students can do justice to themselves in a self-directed piece of coursework. There is unlikely to be the time or space to teach those skills in the busy culture of Year 13. This point can be extended to all subjects, and lies at the heart of the 16–19 tension between creative teaching and learning strategies and assessment-driven imperatives.

However, in A level Geography, the following are presented by Ofsted (2001h) as ineffective teaching strategies and are the kind of traps to be avoided by all 16–19 teachers:

- Note taking (in particular where students have to listen and write at the same time). Better to write up key words on a whiteboard and encourage students to use them in assignments.

- Dictation (disadvantage of being time-consuming and students can mis-hear key terms). Better to use powerpoint slides or OHP slides to provide short summaries of key points.
- Handouts (often go unread). Skeletal notes, which require students to do something to fill them in or to add examples, are more effective in engaging students in what they need to learn.
- Effort given by students to accumulate data with too little then made of it.
- Fieldwork poorly planned.
- Role play games which generate interest amongst students in a topic, but from which few lessons are drawn.
- Pace too brisk for reflection or student contribution.
- ICT use which does not increase geographical knowledge or skills.

Task 15

Consider for a few minutes your own experience of 16–19 teaching. When you were a student yourself, did you hole-punch handouts and file them unread? How might handouts be used more effectively? When teaching yourself, have you resorted to dictated notes? There might be a good justification, but did you ever check the notes students had made? Have you ever put effort into organising a trip for 16–19 students in your own subject only to lose sight of the educational objectives, or allowed students to generate data for a project which is then submitted with no mediation or analysis? If observing 16–19 teaching utilising ICT, was the technology put to good use? Was subject learning (as opposed to skill development) effective?

As contrast, in 16–19 A level English teaching (Ofsted 2001g) the following points are praised:

- Carefully planned oral and written questions, which deepen the grasp of language choices made and reinforce theory and check understanding. It is important that the teacher knows the students' learning needs.
- Well-led plenary discussions which clarify misunderstandings and generate high levels of thinking and response, in which student opinions are valued and students are prompted to put in the effort to think for themselves and gain confidence in handling form and complex language. Teachers can draw on the influence of higher attaining students.
- Build on students' existing insights with well-selected literary criticism which simultaneously develops their ability to read complex material and analyse it.

- Teacher recapitulation of general definitions (especially at the start of AS if students are to apply them confidently later in their course).
- No student is left struggling, yet work is conducted at a challenging pace.
- Is there always something fresh to do? How to fuel a student's appetite for more? How to prompt students to put in an effort to think for themselves, to read a book for themselves?
- Lessons and tasks need to be well organised. The teacher needs to facilitate students working well together in groups or pairs. Beware of using good material (including that from different cultures) with insufficient thought on how to use it to promote demanding work.

Ofsted considers an effective example to be the A level literature lesson in which the skills of note taking were explicitly taught, and the teacher regularly checked notes for usefulness. In this context, students wrestling with a particularly challenging text will do so in the knowledge that later aspects of the lesson will support and deepen understanding. Students should not be thrown in at the deep end too early, and their initial work should not be directionless. Rather it should follow a teacher's framing of key ideas, with teacher intervention at a point where students have (independently) reached a certain point in their understanding, with the aim of moving them forward. Then, carefully planned oral and written questions might guide students to apply a previously introduced idea to three contrasting texts. This supports a deeper grasp of language choices made, and reinforces theory. Well-selected literary criticism can be used in pairs to build on students' existing insights at the same time as developing their ability to read complex material and analyse it. A teacher would complete the lesson by clarifying misunderstandings and leading a plenary discussion to amalgamate lists of important points from individuals or pairs into a composite one.

Thus definitions of effectiveness, at least from an Ofsted perspective and informed by some of the literature, would seem to highlight: subject knowledge, expectations and planning as crucial elements for effective 16–19 teaching. The subject knowledge should be deep enough, broad enough and up-to-date enough to inspire confidence, and should be employed with enthusiasm to stimulate student learning. This might be demonstrated by the thought given by a 16–19 teacher to starting a group in Year 12. The choice of a contemporary text, or one with particular modern resonance like *Frankenstein*, is a preferred start by many English teachers in Year 12.

Expectations should be high, with teachers responding positively to those 16–19 students keen to learn by stretching them. This will help students organise their own learning and understand what they need to do to improve. It will also contribute to a good working relationship. Planning should both structure the teacher guidance and provide opportunities to engage students with theory and practice as appropriate. It should also provide for a clear, accessible bridge between GCSE and AS level work if necessary.

WHAT SUPPORT DO 16–19 TEACHERS NEED TO BE EFFECTIVE?

In a survey reported by Jones (1996), Geography NQTs working in secondary schools particularly enjoyed three aspects of 16–19 teaching:

- the challenging nature of the work in which students were enthusiastic and motivated
- the more personal student/teacher relationship in the context of a friendly classroom atmosphere
- the opportunity to explore an exciting range of teaching strategies drawing on interesting materials with smaller groups.

However, the NQTs reported a number of important issues in relation to their first real experience of 16–19 teaching:

- Difficulty 'handling' students over late essays, poor attendance, chattiness and frictions in group work. This was exacerbated if the NQT were young, suggesting that boundaries in the 16–19 teacher/student relationship need to be defined or redefined. It also suggests a need for students in their own induction into Year 12 to be made clear about expectations of behaviour, learning and studying.
- Resource shortages: some NQTs reported working in departments in which there were not enough 16–19 textbooks, and of schools where they had limited access to school library facilities out of teaching hours. As a consequence, it was difficult to prepare and produce up-to-date teaching materials. This was especially frustrating when NQTs admitted it took them longer to prepare 16–19 lessons.
- Assessment and marking: NQTs reported not really knowing how to mark or when to find the time to mark. This is a thorny issue for all 16–19 teachers. The NQTs found 16–19 assessment difficult and time-consuming, and craved assistance and support in creating marking schemes. The opportunity to double mark with experienced colleagues would have been greatly appreciated. Clearly, internal standardising procedures are important, together with the kind of support provided at Awarding Body briefing and training.
- Subject knowledge: a number of NQTs were anxious about teaching areas of the A level syllabus with which they were unfamiliar. For example, if their first degrees were skewed towards physical or human Geography, they felt significant gaps. This was compounded if (as was invariably the case) NQTs tended not to be given any choice in what they were given to teach, and if they were left to 'get on with' planning, teaching and marking their 16–19 classes.

- Teaching approaches: some NQTs felt constrained by the limited teaching time and the size and nature of the A level specification to be covered. They found it difficult to bring a syllabus to life, to visualise actual lessons and activities from reading the specifications. Many NQTs had a heavy lower-school teaching commitment, and consequently could not give as much attention to 16–19 planning as they wished to. This resulted in new teachers feeling unable to use their vitality, enthusiasm and new ideas to make their 16–19 lessons imaginative. This echoes the concern with assessment-driven constraints on teaching which have grown in early evaluations of the impact of Curriculum 2000.

Support for a more effective initial experience of teaching 16–19 might come from departments or post-16 centres which have a uniform approach to teaching and sharing resources, and agreed strategies for getting students to meet deadlines and behave appropriately in the classroom. This would not require spoon-feeding, or heavy monitoring, but could then enable new 16–19 teachers (and they might not be just NQTs) to be inducted properly, to gain confidence in the 16–19 classroom and hence to build and develop effective teaching strategies.

Task 16

Reflect on your own experience in the 16–19 classroom. When a student yourself, do you recall being stimulated by an enthusiastic teacher who operated in a friendly atmosphere and allowed you to explore learning? If not, did you learn successfully? What lesson do you draw from this?

As a 16–19 teacher have you had to deal with truculent 16 or 17 year olds? Have you successfully managed critical incidents? What do you wish you had done to be a more effective teacher: should you have seen something coming before it happened?

Have you had a chance to work with a colleague to moderate and guide your assessment of 16–19 work? Have you been able to teach a topic (for example at A level) in which you felt confident about subject knowledge? Did it go well? Were there surprises?

If teaching a topic with which you were not especially familiar, were you able to access enough support from a mentor, or colleague (which can of course include lab assistant or librarian)? Would you have preferred to have co-taught a topic in such circumstances?

If in school, have you had to teach a topic while feeling pressures from and loyalty towards lower-school teaching? What support would have made this a more positive experience?

EFFECTIVE TEACHING OF GCSE REPEATS 16–19

The range of teaching groups increasingly available in 16–19 settings necessitates an awareness of different approaches to the purely academic A level and the increasingly academic AVCE. In GCSE English (repeat) it is unsurprisingly reported (Ofsted 2001a) that skilful teaching is required to give students confidence (both those who have not taken it before and those who may be repeating it to attain a higher grade). GCSE work post-16 shares the same criteria as Key Stage 4, but the context of reading passages and topics for writing should, where possible, be tailored to relevant interests and experiences. Approaches need to motivate and secure progress, taking account of the different ability levels and previous experience. Confidence comes from teacher-planned stepping stones for tentative writers.

It is noted that classes can be small, which might seem an advantage to a teacher taking such a group for the first time, but the students can be very challenging to engage and can themselves be demotivated by too small a class. Effective strategies need to include:

- selecting topics of interest they will have views on
- prompting thinking with probing questioning
- taking an imaginative approach, whether to familiar or unfamiliar tasks.

Teachers must plan to make best use of the limited time available (often only two hours a week for eight or nine months). Links with the library can be helpful: drawing on a sufficiently broad book stock, developing supported e-learning, and audio-recording facilities for students' own work, and providing opportunities to practise timed writing tasks.

This can be linked to comments about the other popular resit available in many 16–19 institutions: GCSE Maths, in which as one commentator has observed:

> Teachers find repeat GCSE classes particularly difficult to motivate.
>
> (French 2002, p. 38)

Of critical importance is the need to consolidate exam techniques in relation to GCSE question styles. This must include input to correct misconceptions. It is worth checking if students improve over time in their interpretation of questions. This can be linked to well-defined targets, in which confidence is bolstered through marking aimed to move students on. Crucially, these targets need to be pitched at an appropriate individual level so that all can experience some success. Individual action plans need to be based on honest and informed evaluations of strengths and weaknesses. The other factor (and this is not always present), is the availability of well-structured resources – for work outside the classroom and to sustain motivation.

Whatever approaches are taken, resit students should not be taught as if they were in a class of 15 year olds, but in a way which utilises their wider range of interests and draws on what they are studying on other courses. This is particularly true for vocational GCSEs, for which few school teachers have been adequately trained (Ofsted 2004a).

CONCLUSIONS

It is imperative to facilitate the learning of individuals in 16–19 classrooms by *planning* teaching programmes. This starts with a review of prior learning (which is particularly important to bridge the GCSE/A level gap in Year 12, but is also vital in GCSE resit and vocational teaching, or when taking over a Year 13 group).

Planning involves careful consideration of how to meet student needs. This inevitably necessitates preparation for lessons and sequences of lessons with clear objectives, explicit sequencing and appropriately challenging pace. A key task is to consider how versatile particular groups of 16–19 learners are. Do they vary in ability? Are students 'differently motivated'? It is also important to select and make stimulating learning resources.

Once planned, the process of teaching will be effective if the interactions with students through a diverse range and variety of formal and informal teaching methods can be managed. These could include a repertoire of:

- brainstorming
- presentation by short talk (after which you invite comment and questions)
- demonstration
- questioning
- discussion
- group work to analyse a case study
- simulation
- role-play
- summarising after a group discussion
- problem solving
- feedback to whole group
- lecture.

Such teaching strategies will engage learners if you create a conducive learning environment and manage groups effectively. Evaluation is important. It is worth considering whether the groups you set up are cohesive, and whether all perform the tasks agreed. It is then important to assess outcomes of the session and assess the learning of individuals. Is this what had been planned for?

HEADLINES

- Effective 16–19 teachers are secure in their subject knowledge, and use that to pre-empt student difficulties.
- Effective 16–19 teachers expect students to develop independent learning, but recognise that this needs significant support.
- Effective 16–19 teachers keep checking that what they have planned is understood clearly by all students.
- Effective 16–19 teachers interact purposefully with their students.
- Effective 16–19 teachers stimulate their students' interests and then set targets accordingly.

4   Avoiding preconceptions 16–19: planning for differentiation

Qualifying to Teach Standards

1.6   Understand contribution that support staff and other professionals make to teaching and learning.

3.1.1   Set challenging teaching and learning objectives which are relevant to all pupils in their classes . . . [knowing] the pupils, evidence of their past and current achievement, expected standards for pupils of the relevant age range, range and content of work relevant to pupils in that age range.

3.1.3   Select and prepare resources, and plan for their safe and effective organisation, taking account of pupils' interests and their language and cultural backgrounds, with the help of support staff, where appropriate.

3.3.4   They differentiate their teaching to meet the needs of pupils, including the more able and those with special educational needs. They may have guidance from an experienced teacher, where appropriate.

OBJECTIVES

Reading this chapter and engaging actively with the tasks will enable you to:

- understand why differentiation is crucial to effective 16–19 teaching
- consider teaching strategies to bridge the Year 11/Year 12 gap
- reflect on ways to work with a mentor to challenge preconceptions of 16–19 learners
- implement teaching strategies which will produce evidence to meet QTS Standards 1.6, 3.1.1, 3.1.3, 3.3.4, and FENTO Standards A1–2, B1–3.

FENTO Standards

A: *Assessing learners' needs*
    A1   *identify and plan for the needs of individual students*
    A2   *make an initial assessment of learners' needs*

B: *Planning and preparing teaching and learning programmes for groups and individuals*
    B1   *identify the required outcomes of the learning programme*
    B2   *identify appropriate teaching and learning techniques*
    B3   *enhance access to and participation in the learning programme*

WHY IS IT IMPORTANT TO KNOW LEARNER NEEDS?

To be a really effective teacher in the 16–19 classroom is impossible without knowing students' learning needs. Support for the whole range of needs is a key starting point, after which challenge can be used in an appropriate way to stretch all students. This challenge can come through questions asked at the right time or through a teacher adopting a challenging pace. But challenge is not effective if based on an over-ambitious misconception of what 16–19 learners are (Ofsted 2001l).

If teacher preconceptions lead to premature labelling of 16–19 learners, ineffective planning can result. This can be just as counter-productive as student self-labelling, based on a negative previous learning experience. Both misconceptions can be a powerful barrier in education. An example would be passive 16–19 students rejecting a teacher's misdirected efforts to motivate them. To overcome this, teachers need to be flexible. This flexibility can be planned for, providing that flexibility is overlaid on a stable, supportive and well-organised learning environment.

Students all share a common goal of succeeding in their chosen 16–19 course. This can obviously mean different things for different students, since contexts can be so diverse. But the principle guiding 16–19 teaching must be that students need help and support to enable them to learn, and challenge to enable them to learn effectively. Students have to be taught to learn in the guise of activities to encourage criticality, autonomy and self-direction.

DIFFERENTIATION 16–19

Just as differentiation is considered vital in planning 11–16 teaching, so differentiation is crucial in planning for effective 16–19 teaching. Differentiation is difficult in practice, and is often easier to prescribe than describe. But it can be exemplified by:

- Outcome (Teacher sets a common assessment task to prompt different levels of response). This avoids labelling, and open-ended tasks can have support built in to help weaker students.

- Rate of progress (Student progresses, and accelerates, at his or her own individual speed).
- Enrichment (Teacher provides supplementary tasks or extension work to broaden or deepen individual understanding).
- Set different tasks (Teacher seeks greater sophistication from some students, challenging the brightest within a common theme. At the level of student interaction, different questions can be used, expressed in different vocabulary).

The 16–19 teacher must recognise and take account of the differences in ability, motivation and commitment across the students in their classes, even though they are being prepared for a common exam. Inevitably, given that students have chosen to stay in education, the range will not be completely mixed ability, but an AS level or AVCE class could contain students with GCSE grades in related subjects from D to A★. It could contain students with specific learning difficulties (SLD) such as Attention Deficit Disorder (ADD) or autism, or students with diagnosed or undiagnosed dyslexia. It is crucial that a 16–19 teacher take account of the support available for such students.

Knowing your students' learning needs can also be critical in relation to health and safety and the deployment of adults in the classroom. In Science, if students do not have strong literacy skills, they are unlikely to appreciate all the nuances of written safety advice and procedures during practical work. If students with learning needs are integrated into 16–19 lessons, is provision for Learning Support Assistants integrated into the lesson planning? Is sufficient note taken of students who need to word process notes from classroom teaching straight on to a laptop?

The level of learning support needed by many students can surprise teachers new to 16–19. Some experienced teachers offer workshop sessions or surgeries to their students to underpin developing understanding. However, attendance is often disappointing. Such provision, while extremely well-intentioned, can demonstrate misunderstanding of the stigma a 16–17 year old attaches to voluntary attendance at what looks to them like a 'special' session. Much more effective individual support can be provided by formalised target setting which makes attendance at revision or skills workshops an integrated part of the learning contract in sixth form or college. This can then allow a student's prior life experiences (gender, age, ethnicity, previous educational experience) to be taken into account in a more sensitive way.

There is undoubtedly an issue in 16–19 teaching about how to involve all students. In Sociology, Ofsted (2001q) exemplifies this by describing a hearing-impaired student who relies on word processed notes from his mentor. These are extended at an additional weekly support session. How should a teacher plan for such eventualities in their own 16–19 class? Teachers would agree that any student is entitled to, in this case, a well-balanced study of different traditions, different methodologies and different evidence in Sociology. Yet the teacher needs to think very carefully about formulating questions to enable students of different backgrounds and abilities to demonstrate learning. This will be particularly true for reluctant contributors and those with communicative disabilities. It might involve the compilation of a subject-specific vocabulary list which would benefit all but which would be exceptionally helpful for those students with literacy difficulties. Another example would be for the teacher to target the management of group working very carefully to ensure that all students are included and all contributions are valued.

Differentiation at 16–19 requires the teacher to recognise in their planning that each learner is unique. This is a real challenge for busy teachers, since it involves consideration of three inter-related elements in any lesson:

- the teacher (planning pertinent strategies for all students' needs)
- the learner (who requires the teacher to be clear and the lesson coherent)
- the task (which has to be contextualised in relation to learner needs).

Each learner will have a desired way of understanding the process of education, often an innate preference. Some prefer visual strategies like diagrams, charts, posters, well-designed handouts. Others prefer listening, reading aloud, taping their work. Others favour more active involvement in learning, doing something, even at the level of rewriting their notes. Strategies for learning will involve individuals using specific procedures and techniques. These can be developed, applied and selected by the teacher and provide stimuli to develop capacities across the learning spectrum in any given class. A problem in the 16–19 classroom can be that as teachers we may favour one particular approach. This may be unacknowledged even to ourselves, but it often means our teaching is distorted to favour that one particular approach over all others.

So how can individual needs be met? Coursework can be differentiated at the design stage so that students can choose the level. Worksheets or workbooks can have optional

---

Task 17

Which learning style do you favour in your own professional development?
Do you prefer someone presenting the big picture so you have to make connections, or to have tasks broken down into small steps?
Do you prefer to read things or to listen to them?
Do you like a long initial discussion or to roll your sleeves up and try something out? Think of an example from your own experience: what sort of effect does this have on your approach to 16–19 teaching?

It can be very instructive to ask a colleague to observe you teaching a 16–19 class, and to request feedback on the kind of learning styles your approaches favoured.

sections. Students can be encouraged to volunteer for particular research topics. Peers can be encouraged to support one another's learning, so that areas of confidence can be shared and areas needing further explanation can be explored in their own language. A range of tasks in any particular lesson can be planned for. Whichever approach is taken, support and challenge are crucial.

The 16–19 teacher is faced by a particular dilemma: how to find the right level, both for the group as a whole and for individual students. In a subject like Dance (Ofsted 2002a), students might come on to A level or GNVQ and AVCE courses from very different dance backgrounds. Some will have studied Dance at GCSE and have an understanding of and a commitment to integrating theoretical and practical work in the subject. Others might have come from a 'street dance' performance background and have little experience in writing about dance.

Structured guidance is needed from the teacher to keep expectations high, to stretch individuals and ensure students know what needs to be done to improve. Clarity of expectation and explicit target setting are important, but the most important element in 16–19 classrooms is a good working relationship. This should revolve around the teacher, and enable the under-confident to be encouraged, and the more knowledgeable to contribute in a way that supports learning rather than dominates at the expense of others. This relationship will break down if the teacher's own ideas dominate, and if the teacher stifles student initiative. This is underpinned by ongoing formative and summative comments on assessed work.

In a different way this could be a challenge for the Year 12 teacher in a subject like History. Teaching groups for AS may be widely composed because there is often no requirement for a student to have studied History at GCSE (Ofsted 2001j). Certainly it is important to ascertain if students have studied Humanities or History (or something else entirely) in Years 10 and 11. It is probable that students will have widely different knowledge of periods of history. When it has been established that students have a sound basis in Historical skills and understanding (which could come from a good GCSE grade or from intensive work during the first term of Year 12), then and only then can teachers adopt a more challenging strategy. This could come during discussion, by offering students an exaggerated hypothesis to be intellectually provocative, based on close study of carefully selected documents. A teacher can then, with a confident group of learners, stimulate a more complex level of analysis and argument. However, over-reliance on such a strategy would do little to reinforce the learning of lower attainers, and is ineffective if used to put the unconfident 'on the spot'.

Planning for good practice in 16–19 History teaching might include:

- skilful presentation of up-to-date knowledge to inspire and enthuse (rather than reliance on out-of-date information from a single text book)
- support for students to develop as historians by conducting independent historical investigations rather than teacher spoon-feeding

- encouraging the recognition of different interpretations in the handling of controversial issues through complex sources
- constructive comments on student work which develops accurate use of terminology.

Sometimes very small interventions to differentiate teaching can be effective. An example might be to take account of the needs of weaker students in Year 12 by pausing a video rather than letting it run on in order to allow students to consider the implications of what they have seen, to retain a focus on the aims of the lesson and to correct misconceptions, misunderstandings and lack of engagement. Often this needs to be done subtly on an individual face-to-face basis. This enhances individual student confidence rather than damaging it in front of what might otherwise be a high-achieving class.

To differentiate effectively, it is imperative that 16–19 teachers intervene in sorting out misconceptions in all subjects. Across the sciences, for example, students should have the opportunity to develop skills in sustained arguments, in speculating, in researching for themselves. They need to use scientific ideas, and the teacher needs to be alert to misunderstandings. These should not be left unchecked. If such work does not develop in sophistication through Year 12 and into Year 13, progress is not being made. This is true of practical work too. If students are staying at the level of description and routine handling of results, teachers need to plan for activities which will challenge them to go beyond the superficial. This should include the opportunity to try something and fail, provided that sufficient time is built into the planning for teacher and student evaluation of what went wrong. If those activities remain trivial, or are inefficiently time-consuming, or if students are told what will happen beforehand, there is little chance for teachers to differentiate or to customise their support for individual needs, because those needs may not emerge.

Checking and questioning is crucial at 16–19. If teacher questioning is superficial, (in any subject taught at advanced level) many students will find it difficult to get under the skin of difficult concepts The teacher may be duped into thinking all learners are fully engaged and 'on top of' what has been covered. If excessive notes are laboriously copied, students may lack understanding despite having something to 'show' for being present in a lesson or series of lessons. In the 16–19 classroom especially, teachers need to regularly check the notes their students have taken. This can prove a relatively simple evaluation of how learners are coping. It can also contribute to an ongoing evaluation of the effectiveness of one teaching strategy. In a busy lesson, with pressure on getting through the units, it is easy to neglect.

PLANNING 16–19 EFFECTIVELY

The most effective teaching is likely to engage learners through a range of different approaches, in which discussion and visual stimuli help to break tasks down. Where does a teacher start in this process? Planning at 16–19 involves a teacher focusing down from a set of specifications provided by the Awarding Body. These are the crucial starting point, describing an outline of content and a timeframe, leading to the assessment that students need to encounter during their course.

From this comes a scheme of work, which is usually generated at the departmental level. This will break down and schedule the content into manageable teaching chunks. This is likely to include recommended teaching methods, resources to be used and assessment to be utilised. This will all be framed in a given timescale, which will take account of all that has to be covered on the specification. This all sounds very directed, with little room for creativity or personal interpretation. However, for the individual 16–19 teacher there is still space for professional autonomy through choice of modules, selection of tasks or resources, and it is at the level of discrete lesson planning that effective teaching really comes into its own.

Ideally each 16–19 teacher has a set of objectives which each lesson will aim to meet. These objectives will take account of the broader context in which the lesson is taking place, and out of them will come activities, assessment opportunities (both formative and summative) and resource requirements. Objectives will be a clear statement of instructional intent. It is good practice to visually reinforce them on the board and evaluate them at the end. The most effective objectives are likely to include both behavioural aspects, in which a demonstrable skill is taught, and cognitive, in which broader learning and understanding takes place.

An established strategy to engage 16–19 learners is to be absolutely clear what a good AS or A2 answer should look like. Sensitively chosen and anonymised examples of previous work can play a useful role, particularly if students can discuss marking criteria and attempt to grade the work themselves. This can be followed through with close peer evaluation of students' current work. Standardising exemplars provided by the Awarding Bodies can also be put to good use.

Without effective planning, the 16–19 lesson can be taught in an unconfident manner, with precious teaching time poorly organised (and therefore often wasted). Poor planning can leave students without a clear learning framework, leaving them to question:

- why are we doing this?
- what do we need to learn from this?
- how does it fit with what we have done before so we can build on that?
- how does it link to what we will do next week?

The important point about planning for 16–19 teaching is that the breadth of possibilities is often not exploited by teachers. We can stick to what we know (sometimes regardless of whether it works or not).

Task 18

Which of these did you use in your last 16–19 lesson?
Which are you planning to use in your next 16–19 lesson?

Lead lecture
Short presentation
Discussion
Questions and answers
Seminar
Group work
Brainstorming
Problem solving in teams
Research groups
Role plays
Visits or field trips
Individual tutorials
Individual research
Practicals
Demonstration

Reflect upon what this says about how you plan to assign control: *will your choice of strategies retain control of the lesson entirely? To what extent will you share control with the students in the class? Will you give it over to the students entirely? What will be most effective for your students' learning? Why is this? How much is limited by 16–19 assessment demands?*

Lacklustre teaching can result from inadequate preparation. This is critical in the 16–19 classroom because, without clear-sighted planning, it is impossible to gear activities to individual needs when individual strengths are unknown. Student perception and motivation are important, and time appears so limited. In Art and Design (Ofsted 2001b), teachers are encouraged to plan for students to engage with a broad range of media and a broad range of contexts. Repetitive projects with little scope for the imagination are to be avoided, while trips or visits are recommended as an important part of the 16–19 learning experience. It is worth emphasising that they are only regarded as effective if clear expectations about learning outcomes are made to students.

In Design and Technology too, Ofsted reports (2001e) that teachers must plan for their students to recognise and use the knowledge and skills from previous work in new situations. If teachers can plan to use copies of previous students' work to illustrate the level expected, and what to aim at, demonstrations and explanations at the appropriate level can then be confidently given. Design and Technology teachers at 16–19 are also recommended to factor into their planning an explicit instruction to prevent students spending excessive time on the presentation of their folders. This may be applicable to coursework in other subjects too.

Planning ahead is terribly important if the group is a small one. From the outside, small-group teaching can look like an ideal teaching opportunity, but often it can prove a hard and unrewarding experience for both teacher and students. The latter can remain passive. The result of inadequate planning in such circumstances can be a slow pace in which precious 16–19 teaching time is not well used. It is also likely to lead to the teacher doing far too much talking, and 'telling' students rather than getting students to learn. This can be exemplified in the small Physics group in which half the students are not studying Maths at an advanced level. How can the teacher differentiate in such circumstances, without careful planning to take account of individual need?

One final thought. Teachers are becoming much more confident in using ICT to support their 16–19 teaching (see Chapter 7). But, is the use of ICT in 16–19 lessons always planned for effectively? With an activity like data logging in Science, is accuracy increased, and is time saved, by the indiscriminate use of ICT? In Design and Technology, if planning for ICT use looks over-complex, and for no clear reason, is its use effective? If you have access to an interactive white board, do you plan its use for genuine interactivity?

BRIDGING THE YEAR 11/YEAR 12 GAP

One theme is constantly reiterated in Ofsted reports and in conversations with 16–19 teachers. This is that one of the most important tasks for the 16–19 teacher is to bridge the gap between Year 11 GCSE work with its associated 'learner attitudes', and Year 12 advanced level work with its more demanding standards. For students embarking on study in Year 12, this gap can manifest itself in a culture shock causing lack of confidence as learners struggle with the transition to AS or AVCE level work.

A number of examples can illustrate different aspects of this gap. In a subject within the Science discipline, a teacher needs to be acutely alert to previous attainment across the whole Year 12 class. If there is evidence of strong previous attainment across the group (which is likely to mean a preponderence of A and A★ grades at GCSE), there is little point in setting out to re-teach GCSE topics, which will simply appear trivial and will disappoint (and bore) high fliers. However, if grades are lowish (which is likely to include a preponderence of C and some B and D grades), it is important not to pitch lessons too high at the start of Year 12. The gap has to be bridged in an appropriate way.

Whatever their previous attainment, students should not be left to sink or swim at the start of Year 12. Inexperienced 16–19 teacher preconceptions, which can be uninformed, could make it likely that work is pitched at the wrong level (usually too high for student understanding). Effective use needs to be made of ALIS data (predicting A level grade targets from a spread of previous GCSE scores, with some social factors taken into account).

Task 19

Ask a senior colleague about ALIS data. What data do you have on your 16–19 students? How do you use it to support effective planning?

Insight into that gap between GCSE and advanced work is crucial to making an effective start with a new group of learners. Again in Science, practical work in 16–19 lab sessions can also present problems that have not been apparent previously. Is investigative work integrated with theory, or is theory presented in an indigestible way? And if students have to retake modules or units, is the practical element planned for? Again, the timeframe within which the school or college year is constructed can be inflexible, and so expectations about what is possible may have to be relatively limited.

Subject-specific and discipline-specific misconceptions abound at the start of Year 12. In Modern Foreign Languages, the transition to 16+ learning is reported to be particularly steep (Ofsted 2001m). Have students embarking on AS level in French, German or Spanish gained a clear insight into grammatical structures from their GCSE work? Do they view study of languages at advanced level as a gateway to culture and communication? Teacher planning for some kind of bridging unit between GCSE and the demands of AS can be vital to avoid scaring off otherwise competent and diligent linguists.

In the 16–19 phase, Media Studies at AS, A2, GNVQ and AVCE, and Communication Studies at AS and A2, continue to attract a very wide range of students. This is partly because, as relatively new subjects, many students may not have studied them at GCSE. They also carry a high 'visibility' profile, with media-related jobs and media-related study in Higher Education enjoying immense popularity amongst the age group. It is also perhaps not without significance that AS in both subjects is awarded for 40 per cent coursework. This might look tempting to students who have not experienced unqualified success in their GCSE examinations. Potentially, this presents problems for a teacher, in that planning should be undertaken in the context of building on the skills, knowledge and understanding gained in various ways during KS4. How does a teacher decide how to pitch the lesson or sequence of lessons? How to avoid aiming too low or too high? The resource implications linked to such subjects can be significant: teachers are introducing new material and demanding a new way of analysing material virtually from scratch. This is also true of a subject like Psychology, which can surprise many students embarking on the subject for the first time who have not appreciated the scientific element.

Ofsted (2001l) reported on 16–19 Media courses as attracting more than their fair share of 'low attainers'. This clear need for differentiation might cover students who had gained below a grade C in English GCSE, those who had a thin spread of success at GCSE, those students from a Special Educational Needs background, and those for whom English is an additional language. The recommendation is for direct teaching and explicit interventions to support the learning needs of all, including low attainers in 16–19 classrooms. However, in courses like AVCE Media, featuring important practical components, an interesting tension can develop, for teachers need to step aside and allow students to take charge in activities like video production. In these instances, it may be effective to plan to draw on the contributions from high attainers to support their peers. This has to be underpinned by teacher support for good relationships in the classroom.

In 16–19 English too, despite common entrance standards at C and above for GCSE, there is still likely to be considerable variation from student to student. With the advent of AS specifications, and the broadening of opportunity derived from Curriculum 2000, the size and diversity of Year 12 English classes has increased still further with additional students taking English as their fourth subject. This makes it more important than ever to match texts, tasks and teaching to previous attainment. As all English students need to develop good research skills if they are to succeed, it is imperative that teachers are aware of learner needs, and that they plan accordingly, with high expectations even for lower achievers, and planning to ensure that the very able students make appropriate progress. It is also important, with a rapid rise in the popularity of English Language, and English Language and Literature, A levels, that teachers plan with an insight into what students have learned about language at GCSE, and explain the continuity and discontinuity between GCSE and A level so that learners are not disappointed.

In the range of Business Education courses available at 16–19, less than half the students signing up are likely to have followed any Business-related course in KS4. How can teachers take account of this inequitable starting point? Do some students simply have to mark time at the start of Year 12? Differentiation needs to take place when students are analysing business data as well as collecting it. In Business Education, teacher links with the commercial world are extremely important. Work experience (Ofsted 2001c) should be a well-planned and well-organised extension of the 16–19 classroom. This can be linked to group visits out, and visitors coming in as consultants, mentors and assessors. If students (especially on a vocational course) have a clear work-related ambition, is a teacher able to integrate that fully into a work placement which will need to be planned just as carefully as a sequence of lessons? Such thinking can help teachers to bridge the Year11/Year 12 gap.

In many subjects (a good example is Sociology) it is important to link work to current events. Of course in itself this is difficult to plan for, but teachers need to be flexible, and to consider how a specific newspaper report, television broadcast or outside visit can be utilised fully for its sociological implications. This is an important approach across all subjects, as contemporary, newsworthy exemplifications can add relevance, topicality and interest to the dullest topic at the start of Year 12. There are of course issues with how far this can be taken. With module structures and exam timeframes to take into account, teacher planning is crucial to exploit such opportunities as do occur.

Topical issues can also stimulate and support a teacher's differentiation when starting a subject like Government and Politics (Ofsted 2001i). Not only does a teacher need to plan up-to-date resources by engaging with the real world of politics (for example by gathering information packs from political parties and lobby groups). They also need to organise student attendance at relevant meetings and trips to conferences run by national subject organisations. And perhaps most important of all, they need to work with colleagues in the library to develop a full and up-to-date set of press cuttings.

'SHATTERED ILLUSIONS': WHAT EXPECTATIONS DO TRAINEE TEACHERS HAVE OF 16–19 TEACHING?

Why is all this planning for differentiation necessary? In the run-up to the introduction of Curriculum 2000 (Butcher 2002, 2003a), trainee teachers shared perceptions and expectations about 16–19 teaching. A key issue emerged as the discomfort some trainee or new teachers might expect in their early experiences of 16–19 teaching. This might be attributed to the limited training offered in the 16–19 phase, or the inconsistent approach to 16–19 teaching in some partner schools. Like them, some of you may be in awe of the mystique of A level. Others might struggle to build bridges for pupils between GCSE study in Year 11 and A level study in Year 12. This can lead to the shattering of illusions about 16–19 teaching by the initial experience during training.

Over-expectations might be due to a misplaced assumption that smaller groups of learners, who have chosen to stay on, will already have a desire to learn and a level of motivation. For a teacher new to 16–19, assuming that students will be like keen undergraduates can be a recipe for disaster. Many students moving into the 16–19 phase are likely to lack maturity in their approach to learning, and to be frightened of making fools of themselves in a classroom. They need support before they can start thinking for themselves, and this will involve getting to know their 16–19 teacher a little before being drowned with complex ideas or demanding work. In other words, they may start as 16–19 students expecting everything to be spelt out for them. Although many students will have enjoyed success in Year 11, experienced 16–19 teachers acknowledge that this is often not a preparation for advanced level study. It is your job to wean them gradually from that dependency on spoon-feeding which many will have been used to from GCSE.

So the gap between expectation of 16–19 learners and actuality can be a profound one. A pressing issue for Initial Teacher Training is that mentors need to support and challenge their trainees in the 16–19 classroom in order to close that gap between expectation and reality. Observing experienced 16–19 teachers in the classroom may reveal an unexpectedly high level of explicit teacher guidance to students and a tendency for A level lessons to be teacher led. While this may confirm what Macfarlane (1993) argues about the comfort zone of didactic teaching post-16, it is equally the pressure of AS examinations at the end of Year 12.

It is possible neither the ITT course nor the school-based training touches sufficiently upon appropriate and effective models of 16–19 teaching and learning. As a trainee, you might expect an easier time with your 16–19 teaching than you actually get, and indeed a different relationship in the classroom. The latter, in particular, has to be worked at. The stereotype of 16–19 teaching as smaller groups with few discipline problems and more discussion needs to be challenged. While many students may be quite high academic ability, not all will be. So 16–19 teachers have to work hard in their planning to differentiate, and to support those students struggling with the early demands of A level.

In ITT, discussions with mentors do not always prepare trainees for the reality of sixth-form teaching. Unfortunately the academic literature is thin on analysis of the wide ability range of students studying 16–19, particularly in A level classes. Daw (1996) mentions in his study of successful A level English departments that the less gifted pupils suffer if teachers do not differentiate sufficiently, and Stanton and Richardson (1997) acknowledge the diverse needs of 16–19 students. However, research suggests that trainees can begin 16–19 teaching in ignorance of the breadth of capabilities they might encounter.

As a trainee secondary teacher commented:

> I approached Year 12 texts thinking I was going to share ideas rather than teach. I thought we would be at the same level . . . but it's almost continuing with GCSE. . . . as a trainee teacher I thought that my role was not to be a facilitator but to be a learner with them. . . . I thought having chosen to stay on, they wouldn't be able to stop themselves.

It is too easy to assume 16–19 students are more committed than they actually are. If you rely on open questioning and relatively unclear tasks with no explicit notion of time allowance, the result is likely to be a lesson leaving the majority of the class unenthused, and the teacher working harder than the students. The needs of 16–19 learners have to be recognised in planning.

WHAT CAN MENTORS DO TO CHALLENGE PRECONCEPTIONS?

> Year 12 students so lack in confidence, in speaking, voicing their own views. Very often trainee teachers tend to put them on the spot too much and they are too lacking in confidence to cope with that. . . . Without a little group work before they are put on the spot they get frozen with fear and they won't speak. . . . A lot of new teachers to A level just concentrate on going through a text. . . . Trainees can't see the wood for the trees. . . . It's very difficult to teach students to analyse . . . very bright students have those skills automatically, but the weaker ones don't acquire them without having been taught.

This (English) mentor's comment suggests fertile ground for some challenging interventions in getting trainees to reflect on the 16–19 teaching strategies that might work more effectively than the undergraduate model they drew upon. Unfortunately, the kind of mentor support and training necessary for effective 16–19 teaching can be difficult to achieve in both secondary school and college settings. Even in situations where there are opportunities for mentor engagement with a trainee's 16–19 experience, and even if a mentor employs a warm tone, with plenty of positive eye contact, and asks lots of prompt questions following up abundantly completed observation sheets, a training discussion can still be unhelpful. Haggarty (1995) and McNally and Martin (1998) note the superiority in the power relationship possessed by some mentors. Even if a trainee's stilted acknowledgements of shortcomings are recognised, they can be drowned in a sea of suggestions which eventually obfuscate any clear targets. And if a trainee does not make notes during a mentor session, it is doubtful how much of a mentor's support and challenge can impact on the trainee.

If, during initial training or the induction year, mentor involvement is absent, imprecise or oppressive in relation to 16–19 teaching, the inexperienced teacher may be put off, and resort to the kind of didactic model described in the literature (for example, Hardman and Williamson 1998). This is particularly important if behaviour is surprisingly challenging (tussles over who sits in which chair or staring out the teacher). Often an inexperienced teacher's guard can be down re these discipline offences. In the end you have to stress if behaviour is unacceptable. You need to reflect: what is my relationship with the sixth form? How far is it different from lower down the school?

This comes back to naïve expectations of 16–19 learners. The far broader range of abilities represented in the 16–19 classroom is recognised in some of the literature (e.g. Stanton and Richardson 1997), but the issue needs to be a topic of mentor/trainee discourse so that more varied teaching strategies are encouraged and planning is pitched at an appropriately differentiated level. This can include: sorting out what they had done at GCSE and using very structured small group work to get Year 12 pupils to talk. If trainee teachers come part way through a term, they do not know what preparation has been done and this can exacerbate 16–19 teaching tensions.

Regrettably, neither the Standards for secondary QTS, nor the academic literature, pay sufficient attention to ensuring that trainees are aware of the pitfalls of 16–19 teaching. Hence, the mentor role is even more important. Mentors need to suggest suitable strategies through training.

> Post-16 pupils think they have done it all because they have done one set of major exams. They seem to think that they are experts in all the fields . . . our job is to bridge that. . . . You are trying to develop an individual to be responsible for themselves. . . . Many times we get post-16 pupils who have not actually achieved independent working. . . . We now have pupils trying to do A levels or other post-16 courses that 20 years ago they wouldn't have been considered for.

This valuable mentor insight is exactly the sort of input that trainees need, but it is rare for mentors to be in a position to prioritise this level of critical reflection about 16–19 teaching. These mentor insights are relevant examples of the kind of 'practical knowledge' (Zanting 2001) which trainees benefit from receiving.

> It is absolutely true that most trainees come in expecting to teach maybe at undergraduate level or a little below, and have to reassess the situation. . . . It seems an assumption that post-16 pupils have chosen to stay on at school, so therefore they are going to be motivated. . . . There is a big difference between a student new to post-16 and somebody who has been doing it for a year.
>
> (PGCE mentor)

Many 16–19 students take a considerable time to find the right 'level'. Realising this could be of potential benefit to trainee teachers and NQTs in enhancing Year 12 responsiveness, by making students feel included rather than excluded. If, through the training dialogue, mentors empower trainees to give real attention to the specific learning needs in Year 12, differentiation in the sixth form, separating the fact that students all have to do the same exam from the tendency to give them all the same homework, could be more effective.

It would certainly be helpful if mentors felt able to challenge their trainee's preconceptions of post-16 teaching early on, in order to reduce or prevent awkward, unsatisfying and ineffective 16–19 teaching experiences, from which little positive is learned. If intervention was timed to impact on trainees' planning for Year 12 teaching and supported through genuine experience of Year 13 teaching, a clearer, more informed picture of 16–19 teaching would develop for trainees. This would have a positive effect on secondary NQTs' confidence in the 16–19 classroom.

WHAT CAN MENTORS DO TO SUPPORT 16–19 DIFFERENTIATION?

As with any aspect of a teaching practice, you may experience problems with rapport in the 16–19 classroom as students adjust to the change of teacher. However, mentors can play a crucial role in supporting trainee teachers as they explore differentiation in the 16–19 classroom. There is a dilemma, with on the one hand, trainees assuming 16–19 student capability to be high and academically motivated. Hence you plan for interactive and discussion-based lessons. On the other hand, reality can be experienced very differently, with 16–19 students revealed as possessing a far wider spectrum of abilities and motivations than had been assumed, as shown in the insecurity of their responses. You are not likely to be effective in the 16–19 classroom if you aim only for the highest attainers.

The work of Higham (1996) and Watts and Young (1997) highlights the connection between the narrow curriculum post-16 and the teaching approaches adopted, leading to opportunities in post-16 education being severely limited except for the upper ability range. The dilemma is an important topic for mentors to confront and support in their training role, even more so now that the time pressures of Curriculum 2000 impinge upon 16–19 teachers.

It must be understood that the need for differentiation does not stop at 16. Discussions about differentiation 16–19, part of an active role for mentor intervention, are particularly pertinent when trainees are given (understandably in some contexts) a relatively limited experience of 16–19 teaching. Many trainees foresee difficulties getting sufficient post-16 experience, so the NQT year can broach new territory rather than providing an opportunity to consolidate.

The mentor management role in the partner school can be crucial to ensure any partnership includes sufficient training in post-16 teaching. The situation would obviously be different for a trainee in a sixth-form college or FE college environment. Trainees are then able to work with a broader range of post-16 classes, enlightening perceptions about the confidence of many Year 13 students.

Naturally, over a two-year A level course students develop in confidence and learn vital independent study skills. This is an important factor, for if you are denied access to a full range of 16–19 teaching, you will need to know what Year 12 students are working towards. A partial picture does not aid ability to plan appropriately differentiated classes.

Researchers report a prevalence of what might be called 'hands-off' mentoring 16–19. This is a shame, as 'informing' mentor/trainee conversations prior to 16–19 teaching commencing can be effective. For example, it takes a while for a 16–19 group to feel comfortable enough to relax with you, and groups need quite a lot of guidance to start with. Without mentor involvement, 16–19 students who crave empathy and warmth (Harkin *et al.* 2001) could remain unconfident and uninvolved in your classes. You may resort to intensive and active attempts at motivation, to be fluid and use brainstorming a lot to develop ideas and keep pushing students. But this degree of activity and flexibility from the 16–19 teacher can be exhausting, and in the end does not always result in effective learning.

Some trainee teachers will of course find their own strategies without mentor involvement. However this is a risk in an intensive course of initial teacher training, in which a sink-or-swim approach would not be acceptable pre-16. It is also a concern that unmediated approaches to 16–19 teaching could have a very negative effect on student learning. For example, you may resort to the same sixth-form teaching strategy as was used on you, which might be an exclusive diet of teacher-led whole-class discussion.

This is the argument used by Elliott and Calderhead (1995) that trainee teachers draw on their own experience as pupils, in this case sixth formers. It is not difficult to see where misconceptions and surprises arise. Often a 16–19 classroom lay-out is informal, and experienced 16–19 teachers will appear to effortlessly guide debate. However the amount of guidance provided by the teacher and the reluctance or lack of confidence of some students to join debates, the very specifically guided research, and the structured lessons plans followed by the teachers are a much clearer indication of what is necessary for effective 16–19 teaching.

This physical transition of the post-16 classroom represents a break from Year 11. Year 12 lessons often begin with the teacher moving the desks or tables from their previous lecture-style arrangement. The conundrum for trainee teachers confronted with most 16–19 classrooms is that they tend to possess an air of undergraduate informality, as symbolised by a more open room-layout. But many Year 12 students in this informal environment are struggling to handle the transition from Key Stage 4, and lack undergraduate-level skills of independent learning.

Trainee teachers can learn from their mentor, early in their practice, that structured guidance, coming from carefully differentiated planning, is more likely to lead to effective 16–19 teaching. As the literature attests (Macfarlane 1993, Richardson 1993, Bramald et al. 1995), confronted with the problem of assessment and the pressing need to get through the syllabus, many 16–19 teachers seem forced into a more teacher-directed pedagogy. This may be a difficult lesson for trainee teachers to learn without mediation by their mentor. It might also discourage some trainees from innovatory teaching strategies with their 16–19 classes.

A mentor explains the limited attention given to 16–19 teaching thus:

> Often in schools perhaps we take our sixth-form teaching too much for granted because pupils doing A level want to be there, and there are so many initiatives lower down the school that have to be seen to. . . . I think the focus will change again because with modular A levels there will be a huge focus on structuring sixth-form courses and looking at subject matter and methods of delivery. . . . But it may become more difficult for student teachers to access sixth-form teaching because schools will be very anxious . . . it is difficult to give trainees public examination classes.

There are three important points raised here:

- First, if schools do take their 16–19 teaching for granted, it places an even greater onus on the mentor to draw out relevant issues for any trainee, rather than leave them to their own devices.
- Second, trainees need to reflect even more carefully on 16–19 teaching when the pressure of assessment at the end of Year 12 can have a deleterious effect on pedagogy.
- Third, if it is less easy for trainees to experience 16–19 teaching during their training, the dangers of a vicious cycle of cursory attention to the needs of tertiary learners could become embedded in ITT.

The literature suggests that A levels (Pound 1998) and, in a different way GNVQ (Butcher 1998), can offer new ways of learning for 16–19 students, yet trainee teachers can struggle to find their own way of dealing with this. This can have a significant impact, when for many the vast majority of their time in school is spent working in Key Stages 3 and 4. There are two issues for mentors. The first is how to support trainees to differentiate at Year 12 in order to facilitate progression from Year 11. The second is how to offer any clarity about the differentiation from Year 12 to Year 13, which seems generally absent but which would enable trainees to see a fuller picture of where they were going with Year 12s.

Mentors also need to be pro-active in engaging with, and if necessary challenging models of post-16 teaching drawn from a trainee's own experience of being in sixth forms themselves, or models developed from emulating the behaviour of observed teachers. If you observe popular post-16 teachers in action, blending thinking aloud with a judicious mix of writing down and direct questioning and sounding authoritative, it may be at a lower level than you expect. It needs structuring this much to accommodate the range of abilities now attracted to 16–19 education.

Learning to teach in secondary schools is challenging enough for trainees without additional struggles and stresses from 16–19 teaching. The most effective mentors do manage to be highly supportive in the 16–19 phase despite other professional demands on their time. Regrettably, 'hands-off' 16–19 mentoring can leave trainees to learn to teach in this phase virtually unaided.

CONCLUSION: EVALUATE YOUR PLANNING FOR EFFECTIVE DIFFERENTIATION

It is critical that as a 16–19 teacher you evaluate the effectiveness of your own teaching on the A level, GCSE or AVCE course you teach. This should be a thorough, albeit small-scale evaluation which focuses on two key questions:

- What is the impact of your teaching on the learning of all students in your 16–19 class?

- How might it be improved?

Some teachers new to the 16–19 phase will be concerned at how creativity can be put into teaching when the specifications are so tight. The answer is that even with a pre-designed set of specifications, it is possible to strike a balance between the ideology of the course and your own. Planning is where this engagement happens, with the choosing and rejecting of content, with the selection of a suitable teaching sequence.

When evaluating the effectiveness of any learning process, an important question is whether students have the skills to do the tasks planned for. Students have to be managed in learning how to learn. This places the 16–19 teacher firmly in the role of facilitator, enabling skills, attitudes, concepts and knowledge to be developed. The 16–19 teacher has to emphasise the need for students to develop learner skills, rather than focusing entirely on content. Getting students to grade themselves 1–5 in information–retrieval skills on a regular basis is an effective way to engage 16–19 year olds as learners rather than vessels expecting to be filled.

Task 20

Reflect upon a recent or proposed assignment for your 16–19 students. Use the following prompts to evaluate your awareness of their learning needs.

- What does a student do if asked to 'evaluate'?
- How do they move from a set of class notes to an elegant essay?
- How do they find out more information without wasting their time in inefficient internet searches?
- How do they write or design in a required genre, specific to a particular subject and discipline?
- Can they copy effectively from your writing on the board?
- Can they read a piece of text in the time you give them?
- Can they spell relevant words or key names correctly? (How do you boost the esteem of 16–19 students struggling with spelling? Do you re-test, put errors on post-its, use mnemonics, explain single/double letter confusions?)
- How ideal are your students' notes?
- Do they use highlighting?
- Do they make use of spidergrams or flow charts to aid learning?
- Do they use mind mapping, with a starter sentence in the middle of a page with related ideas thrown down prior to sequencing?
- Can they skim-read passages from text books? (Headings and sub-headings first, then opening sentence, scan for gist by searching for key concepts with highlighter in hand, skimming for specific words.)

Do not forget that, to really differentiate effectively, a 16–19 teacher might want to build rest into their planning. A couple of minutes chilling out in a hectic lesson can keep students energised and engaged. And do not forget it can be counter-productive to give students too much choice, so that some never get to complete the task you have given them.

Differentiated planning, based on a realistic understanding of the needs of 16–19 students, is the first building block to effective teaching.

HEADLINES

Three factors to take into account when planning for differentiation 16–19:

- 16–19 students vary in their existing subject knowledge, in their attainment, and in their approach to study skills.
- The specifications for 16–19 courses will include content and assessment. Do not muddle the two in your planning.
- Your values as a 16–19 teacher will be informed by the institutional context in which you work, and your own experience and perception of 16–19 education. Be aware of what those values are.

5   Subject expertise in 16–19 teaching

Qualifying to Teach Standards

2.1   *Secure knowledge and understanding of the subject(s) they are trained to teach.*
       d. Aware of the pathways for progression through the 14–19 phase in school, college
       and work-based settings. . . . Familiar with the key skills (QCA) and the national
       qualifications framework. . . . Know the progression within and from their own subject
       and the range of qualifications to which their subject contributes. They understand how
       courses are combined in students' curricula.

3.3.2 *They can teach the required or expected knowledge, understanding and skills relevant*
       to the curriculum for pupils in the age range for which they are trained. . . . Those
       qualifying to teach post-16 pupils teach their specialist subject(s) competently and
       independently using, as relevant . . . programmes specified for national qualifications.
       They also provide opportunities for pupils to develop the key skills specified by the
       QCA.

(FENTO Standards do not include subject expertise)

OBJECTIVES

Reading this chapter and engaging actively with the tasks will enable you to:

- appreciate the importance of subject knowledge in effective 16–19 teaching
- reflect on gaps in students' subject knowledge when they enter the 16–19 phase
- make effective use of subject knowledge support from mentors, colleagues and outside agencies
- implement teaching strategies which will produce evidence to meet QTS Standards 2.1d, 3.3.2.

SUBJECT KNOWLEDGE AS A BASELINE FOR EFFECTIVE TEACHING

It comes as no surprise to learn that subject knowledge is considered an essential component in effective 16–19 teaching. Across all 16–19 disciplines, Ofsted reports consistently emphasise the importance of subject knowledge. Teacher confidence is a significant factor here, with security in the face of 16–19 learners a necessary starting point to develop students as confident learners. This would seem to suggest that the traditional model of a 16–19 teacher as a school-based single-subject expert still prevails.

However, this only tells half the story. While all 16–19 teachers undoubtedly need subject expertise in order to understand specification content and the critical issues within that content, students need to be able to access that subject knowledge and to engage with it in an effective way. This can vary from subject to subject. The curriculum and assessment structures aimed at 16–19 students no longer imply a simple transmission model of teaching, in which an unresponsive didacticism (teachers telling what they know in order to fill students' heads with knowledge) is presented. What teachers know is not necessarily what students need to learn. The wider range of full-time 16–19 students now taking A level and AVCE qualifications, together with advances in our understanding of how learners learn, means that 16–19 subject knowledge needs teacher mediation. With the introduction of Key Skills, teachers need to support students in taking responsibility for their own learning, so they know how to learn as well as what to learn.

There is a real dilemma for 16–19 teachers in relation to subject knowledge. Research suggests their students are motivated by active learning strategies (Harkin *et al.* 2001), but the introduction of added pressure from public examinations in Year 12 creates a tension in which teachers may be wary of losing control if they do not teach from the front. With Year 12 effectively reduced to two terms' teaching and then revision for exams, an understandable fear is of wasting precious time. So how can less confident, less experienced 16–19 teachers be sufficiently assured in their subject expertise that they can start to teach creatively and not be dictated by the threat of looming assessment?

Task 21

A good starting point is to self-assess your own subject knowledge in relation to the A level or AVCE specifications you are expected to teach. Is your subject knowledge:

- Sufficiently detailed?
- Sufficiently up-to-date?

- Deep enough to challenge and elicit confidence in the highest attainers?
- Flexible enough to support the lowest attainers?
- Maintained enthusiastically by being a learner yourself?
- Used to motivate and inspire students?

This kind of self-assessment is best done with an experienced colleague or mentor. Any gaps, or tentativeness, should be addressed as training, induction or appraisal targets.

But remember subject expertise is not clear-cut. Good sixth-form English teaching, for example, is reported to integrate both language and literature objectives (Ofsted 2001a). The most effective 16–19 English teachers use their knowledge of relevant academic disciplines (such as linguistics, literary criticism, literary or social theory or cultural history) to guide students in deepening and extending their response to, and analysis of, texts. Interestingly, Ofsted reports that such scholarship is worn lightly. In other words, 16–19 teachers should carry their subject knowledge naturally, as a resource they can draw upon. They should not have to spend a lesson reading out verbatim from a textbook, or struggling to keep one step ahead of their students. (Of course this can happen with new 16–19 teachers or new A level specifications, but it is not to be recommended as effective practice.)

This exemplification is also apparent in Modern Foreign Languages (Ofsted 2001m) when effectiveness is defined as fluent teachers providing a consistently accurate model to emulate in relation to their own skilful and competent language use.

How is subject expertise exemplified in the 16–19 classroom? Critically, it is reinforced to students in the confident responses to questions that effective 16–19 teachers make, and the ease with which they present the difficult elements in a topic. However, for some 16–19 teachers, there is a danger of being carried away with a showy and pretentious use of subject knowledge which may leave students bamboozled. (This can often be spotted by a glazed or troubled look on students' faces!) If you spot your 16–19 class doing this, come down off those Olympian heights and differentiate your subject knowledge for the benefit of all. Feedback from a colleague who has observed you in action can be very valuable in this instance, especially when an agreed target has been the degree to which students have been engaged by the teaching.

It is worth considering what support there is for your own subject-knowledge development. Is there an active reading community in your department which shares and keeps up to date with current developments in the discipline? Do you talk with colleagues about your subject interests? In English, some effective centres have their own writing communities in which teachers' interests can be fostered. Is there a parallel for your subject?

WHAT IS SUBJECT EXPERTISE?

There is an intriguing debate (see Pring 1995) about whether the kind of knowledge teachers require for teaching at A level ('knowing that') is completely different from, or related to, the knowledge required on vocational courses ('knowing how'). A good example can be found in Geography, where some A level teachers are working in a relatively traditional academic context, yet on the same timetable might be contributing to GNVQ or AVCE Travel and Tourism which requires industrial experience and access to relevant placements. Are they both working at different points on the same learning continuum? Are they both developing skills in their students? How has their training prepared them for utilising such a breadth of subject knowledge?

Unfortunately, the relationship between school or college teachers and subject academics based in universities is not as close as it used to be. Lecturers used to serve as A level examiners, used to write text books, and used to serve on subject associations. With scholarship in higher education interpreted since 1992 as what contributes to the Research Assessment Exercise, most staff in universities are forced, reluctantly in many cases, to turn their backs on the needs of 16–19 students and their teachers. This raises problems in terms of the interplay between cutting-edge knowledge generation in HE and what is presented for 16–19 students. This comes to a head in the ITT standards, which demand confidence in subject knowledge, without making explicit where that knowledge comes from or whether it is 'fixed'. Subject knowledge at 16–19 is thus not without controversy. It is dynamic and changing, and not necessarily the same as the subject knowledge generated in HE to which teachers were exposed as undergraduates.

Subject expertise has an important wider impact on 16–19 education. Maths, for example, has seen a well-publicised decline in the subject as a proportion of the total A level entry. It has also seen decline as a subject taken alongside Science A levels and in combination with Further Maths. It has almost reached the status of an annual media story that we would need every single Maths graduate to enter teaching to even begin to address the shortfall in specialists with 16–19 Maths expertise. What role does teacher subject knowledge have in this decline, or more importantly in arresting this decline? To put it bluntly, how good is your algebra, calculus and vector geometry?

Subject expertise can be demonstrated in different ways in different subjects. In Music, Ofsted reports (2001n) that 16–19 subject knowledge should be modelled by working alongside students, to inspire and motivate across different styles. Examples of effectiveness include musical terminology being used accurately, and the teacher insisting that students use terminology correctly as well. Subject knowledge is particularly important in 16–19 Music when a teacher may be introducing topics like harmony not covered in the GCSE syllabus.

In Sociology, Ofsted (2001q) reports that mastery of subject knowledge for 16–19 has to be allied to fit-for-purpose methods if teaching is to be considered effective. Again, 16–19 teachers must insist on accurate terminology, and encourage the use of

ICT to present findings. A particular concern is whether students are being taught how to interpret numerical data. Teachers are also encouraged to find ways to make 16–19 students practise research and data-collection in order that they can use and evaluate different methodological approaches.

Subject knowledge is reportedly demonstrated by:

- clear and succinct explanation of terms and principles
- explanation of generalisations as well as exceptions and contradictions
- contemporary events used as illustrations
- cross-referencing to different topics studied.

This set of four criteria is applicable across a number of subjects. In Government and Politics for example (Ofsted 2001i), effective 16–19 teachers are reported as providing clearly defined positions in any debate, drawing on detailed research and an underlying enthusiasm. In Geography (Ofsted 2001h), fieldwork studies can (and indeed it is argued should) throw up ethical issues. It needs a well-informed teacher, confident in their subject expertise, to deal with these with confidence. In addition, examiner reports repeatedly comment that student knowledge of physical geography is not as good as human geography. How do 16–19 teachers address that?

Ofsted (2001e) tells us that in Design and Technology, post-Curriculum 2000, six-unit courses have increased the need for subject knowledge and skills in product analysis and industrial practice. This has at least changed, if not broadened, the subject mastery necessary for effective 16–19 teaching. In Art and Design (Ofsted 2001b), teachers are likely to be effective when they have confidence in their own drawing ability and can demonstrate techniques themselves to their students. They are encouraged to forge strong links with local Art Foundation courses, and with the nearest ITT provider, partly to extend possible gallery visits, partly to draw on cultural diversity and partly to keep up to date with progression routes into HE for their students. This is a reminder that 16–19 teachers need to sustain contacts with their subject communities, and to engage in the discourse and (where appropriate) the practice of the subject themselves. This can be supported through membership of subject associations (see end of chapter).

In Drama and Theatre Studies, Ofsted (2001f) again expresses a clear line about the importance of subject knowledge. To be considered effective, a 16–19 teacher should have a fluent and confident knowledge of plays and playwrights and their social and cultural context. In this instance, subject knowledge should include practical skills in acting, directing, design and stagecraft. It should include specialist terminology to demonstrate styles and conventions, and the teaching of written skills of analysis and research skills. It should not feature the over-domination of the teacher's own ideas. This latter point is an important reminder and rejoinder, and supports the idea of learning being worn lightly. Subject expertise should be used to the benefit of all students in 16–19 education.

Subject knowledge requirements can certainly change over time. In Physical Education (Ofsted 2001o), the need for confident and up-to-date subject knowledge to teach effectively in the 16–19 classroom is stronger than ever. No longer are PE teachers in the post-compulsory setting responsible only for non-examined PE. Increasingly, schools and colleges are offering a range of A level, AVCE and GNVQ provision, as well as non-traditional courses like Community Sports Leaders Award. The PE teacher needs to be competent in the technical command of knowledge and skills, including elements drawn from biology, physiology and psychology, teaching them with the appropriate rigour, depth and insight for 16–19 students. They need to be engaged with academic debates around the nature, purpose and coverage of sport.

Media education is a relatively new area for schools and colleges, but the 16–19 subject-knowledge requirements are considerable. Subject expertise at the academic level is expected to cover: representation, language, institutions, values and audiences. This should be used to convey contextual understanding of the media industry. For example, the 16–19 teacher in this subject should have a high standard of language to model analysis, but should not resort to jargon. However, the teacher is not only expected to have up-to-date knowledge of the media industry, but they are also required to be technically skilled to assist students in media production. These skills are not easy to develop and sustain 'on the job', but teacher work-shadowing and work-placement opportunities do come up, so media studies teachers (and others with a need for 'hands-on' subject knowledge) should keep their eyes peeled.

The changes to the specifications for AS and A levels introduced as a result of Curriculum 2000 have had a major impact on subject knowledge. There were new criteria and assessment objectives (and new terminology) common across all Awarding Bodies, and experienced teachers have had to learn to assess coursework according to new criteria and at the different AS and A2 levels.

Organising any subject into three AS modules in year one, and three A2 modules in year two, all of which can be assessed in January or June each year, poses interesting challenges for department heads. For example, coursework elements on the five English Language and Literature, six English Literature and five English Language specifications offer considerable flexibility to teachers. Matters are further complicated in those schools and colleges offering the Intermediate GNVQ or the six-unit AVCE in Media: Communications and Production (formerly Advanced GNVQ), to say nothing of the potential role for 16–19 English teachers in Key Skills (UCAS 2000).

Trainee teachers have no need to be intimate in their understanding of how departments choose to organise 16–19 study opportunities. However, neither would it seem helpful to let anyone loose on 16–19 teaching blissfully unaware of any of the decisions that have been made about what is on offer in their classes. What aspects of their subject are trainees informed about? Is this sufficient to enable them to be effective 16–19 teachers?

TRAINEE TEACHERS' 16–19 SUBJECT KNOWLEDGE

Trainee teachers can sometimes be in a position to confront controversies around subject expertise in the 16–19 classroom. Being a 16–19 teacher of any subject does not necessarily mean the same thing to every individual, and the personal and subjective elements present in every subject means they can lack uniformity. As a result, trainee teachers can confuse intention and purpose in their thinking. This conundrum over subject knowledge may be a generic problem, relevant to all teachers new to 16–19 teaching. Does the expertise they have gained in success at degree-level study fit the requirements for their subject at A level or AVCE? To reiterate a crucial question: is what they know what 16–19 learners need to know?

In English, for example (Butcher 2003b), secondary trainees view the subject as representing the most contested subject ideology amongst practitioners in schools and colleges. Many trainees tend to enter English teaching with a passionate love of literature, yet the English they encounter in school placement represents what Goodwyn (1997) calls an antithesis between different models.

English is an intriguing example because it has been prey to government diktat in a number of areas of compulsory education (for example the imposition of the National Literacy Strategy, or the use of Standard English in the National Curriculum). This suggests that the subject has been under external scrutiny and in crisis for the last twenty years, principally over what counts as knowledge, what attitudes and values are embedded in the subject, and who has control of the literary canon. But English is not unique. Is there any sense of your subject 'settling down'? Will it ever? So how do trainees engage with these debates, and how do these debates affect assessment of competence in ITT? If subject knowledge really is important in effective 16–19 teaching, yet there is dispute over what that subject knowledge is, new teachers in particular are placed in an invidious position in the 16–19 classroom. How can teachers exploit their subject knowledge to enjoy the possibility of autonomy in 16–19 teaching?

The problematic nature of defining English in terms of subject knowledge (Dart and Drake 1996) is fuelled by a schism between teachers trained in different subject beliefs. Of course most teachers operate somewhere between the two, and many can hold two seemingly contradictory beliefs quite happily as they pursue the Curriculum 2000 assessment objectives.

Inevitably, beliefs about subject knowledge affect approaches to teaching. Do your beliefs about your subject favour a didactic pedagogy 16–19, or a constructivist generation of pupil knowledge? In 16–19 classrooms, where teachers have retained some limited power over the curriculum, and where pedagogy is usually less affected by the need to keep control, the potential for heartfelt disagreement about subject knowledge is more exposed.

For trainee teachers, the differing philosophies could lead to differing interpretations of the ITT Standards by mentors, expressed in differing subject discourses and even possible failure. Such departmental cultures are contextualised in relation to these subject debates in Arthur *et al.* (1997).

It has also been reported in a study of Maths and English trainees (Drake and Dart 1997) that any firmly held beliefs about the subject that mentors hold need to be shared with, and made explicit, to the trainee. In the example they quote, a mentor and a student had a complete disagreement over the trainee's attitude in the post-16 classroom and subsequently how she was assessed. As a result she had to be moved to another school. The problem centred on the trainee's alleged failure to enthuse pupils by making overt her love of her subject in a way which the mentor judged important in relation to the Standards. This suggests a need for mentors to articulate their beliefs and values about the subject, in order to deliberately make their students think through their own positions, beliefs and values.

However, are mentors reluctant to engage in discussion about the nature of any subject? Davies (1993, 1997) reports mentors avoiding the contentious nature of English, even when prompted by student teachers. The potential conflict is further exacerbated by Ofsted possessing a very fixed view of the kind of ITT curriculum that PGCE students should follow, which may or may not coincide with mentor perceptions of the subject.

In Dart and Drake (1996) the mismatch between trainee teachers' pre-PGCE subject experience is problematised. This includes (for English trainees) the kind of literature studied and valued, and mentors' perception of the subject as influenced by syllabus choices. Trainee teachers were reported as tending to fall back on their own experience as learners, culminating at worst in an uncritically espoused love of literature. However, as Arthur *et al.* (1997) claim, a trainee teacher's view of their subject will inevitably impact on their choice of teaching strategies. Looking for support and modelling of effective practice from their mentor, they are likely to find, as Bloomer (1997) describes, great variation in pedagogic practices 16–19.

Daw (1996) helpfully isolates the factors contributing to academically successful A level English teaching. These could be generalized for all 16–19 teaching to include:

- the subject expertise of staff
- the commitment of staff
- the balance of teaching methods
- pupil experience of challenging teaching in their subject at KS4
- teacher recognition of the depth of knowledge required to introduce topics with confidence (which now means a focus on assessment objectives and sharing these with students)
- departments which do not assume all teachers could automatically teach at this level without support and training
- the importance of pupils' cultural capital, whether gained from school or home.

Of particular significance is his concern that the less gifted post-16 pupils suffer if teacher expectations are not sufficiently differentiated.

What seems to be missing from Daw's list is the importance of understanding student perspectives on learning. This is corrected by Harkin *et al.* (2001) who provide evidence of what post-16 students value (autonomy). Whatever sort of 16–19 students a trainee or inexperienced teacher encounters, the debate over subject knowledge in all 16–19 classrooms is an important one. To develop effective deployment of subject knowledge needs dialogue with more experienced colleagues. This is particularly important given the limited coverage directly related to teaching 16–19 on most secondary PGCE courses.

For trainee teachers, it is worth reflecting back with a mentor on the mentor's own difficult and stressful experience of teacher education, to establish if they felt under-prepared for 16–19 teaching, and to utilise this as a resource to establish common ground. Most departments, whatever their subject, find intelligently critical trainee teachers a valuable stimulus to current practice. Mentors can use the Standards (TTA 2002) from an early stage to develop conversations about subject knowledge for 16–19 teaching and as a diagnostic element. This should present a positive opening, since trainees share with their mentors a background in some areas of the subject, and a professional aim of teaching their subject as effectively as possible in the 16–19 classroom. Without these discussions about 16–19 subject knowledge, opportunities can be lost to develop really effective 16–19 teaching skills.

WHY IS SUBJECT KNOWLEDGE A PROBLEM IN YEAR 12?

Secondary trainees often express disappointment in relation to subject knowledge on first teaching Year 12 AS classes. Trainees are surprised at the lack of technical language, at the weak critical skills, and at the narrow cultural capital displayed by students. They assumed all three would be far more advanced in students choosing to start an academic 16–19 course. This preconception judged that skills of critical analysis, informed by an appropriate technical vocabulary and a degree of cultural awareness, were vital for success in A level. This tallies with Daw's (1996) analysis of successful A level English departments. But the need to differentiate subject knowledge in 16–19 classrooms can be a real jolt to trainees' beliefs about teaching in that phase. Do you think A level has a mystique which makes students uncomfortable voicing their opinions? Are you surprised how much prompting and encouragement 16–19 students needed?

Do you find, in particular, the limited range of subject vocabulary possessed by the students who had, a few months previously, succeeded at GCSE, disconcerting? Do you have to make more allowances than you'd expected to make?

The issue of cultural capital raised by Daw (1996) is significant. Some 16–19 students will seem incapable of answering your questions and the level of response can bump you right down to earth. It is worth asking yourself when you actually acquired all that subject knowledge. Have you forgotten what it was like in Year 12?

Mentors usually agree that trainee teachers and NQTs often make inappropriate assumptions about 16–19 students, equating them with undergraduate-level students. Unfortunately, this misreading can remain unchallenged if there is an absence of effective pre-placement discussion or guided observation when training in the 16–19 classroom.

The crucial point here is that inexperienced 16–19 teachers need to be alerted explicitly that GCSE can provide for many students an inadequate foundation in the skills required for success in A Level (which is closely correlated to the challenge of the GCSE experience).

Are your Year 12 students made aware of the different study skills required for A level? Do they see A levels as an easy option, even though such a different approach is needed and success at GCSE does not guarantee even a pass at A level? Inexperienced teachers can be forced to find their own strategies to attempt to teach A level effectively and bridge those subject-knowledge gaps.

This leap from GCSE to A level study is recognised across all subject disciplines. The impact of this gap is profound on Year 12 students, with many reported as struggling to cope with the analytical skills and cultural/scientific reference points apparently necessary for success. Inexperienced teachers can have their confidence destabilised in encountering such a mismatch between their subject knowledge and what is known (or not known) by many 16–19 students.

Unfortunately, due to pressure on Year 13 teaching to prepare students for A2 exams, inexperienced teachers often have a 16–19 teaching experience limited to Year 12. As a consequence, they are unable to see the intellectual and affective developments that take place for many students over the course of two or three years' full-time study. Being able to reflect upon the enhanced A2 subject knowledge gained across a Year 13 class would help teachers struggling to cope with weak subject knowledge amongst students in Year 12. However, Year 13 is regarded as sacrosanct by many experienced teachers and schools, mindful perhaps of the impact in the local community of A level grades. Some sort of shadowing or team-teaching arrangement for Year 13 could be highly beneficial to inexperienced 16–19 teachers.

One consistent undercurrent from trainee teachers privileged enough to access Year 13 teaching has been the recognition that Year 13 students are far more mature and confident in their critical skills than their Year 12 counterparts. This is an important reminder, if you are struggling with passive Year 12 groups, that there is light at the end of the tunnel. What is regrettable is that so few trainees get to see this transformation, and that it is under-reported in the literature. If trainees did gain fuller access, they might be clearer in their understanding that Year 13 pupils possess these subject-related skills, not by some magical process associated with being in Year 13, but because they have been taught them in Year 12, and are able to apply what they have learned with greater sophistication.

WHEN IS SUBJECT KNOWLEDGE A PROBLEM?

In 16–19 education an increasing number of subjects fall outside established boundaries and initial training. When schools in particular are opening up vocational alternatives utilising existing staff, or are moving into new A level disciplines, how are the teachers of such subjects to be developed? For example, A level English Language offers significant subject-knowledge challenges to most trainee English teachers, yet A level English Language is an increasingly popular option, and represents a relatively new area with which English teachers need to familiarise themselves. There may be parallels in other disciplines. So does the view that 16–19 teaching is purely about single-discipline teaching remain true? This is not only demonstrably false, but it is also one area of opportunity and expertise that could differentiate any search for a teaching post.

Subjects that have not been taught in the 11–16 National Curriculum are interesting examples because trainees recognise that Year 12 students can have an inappropriate expectation about what the subject would be like at A level. This means it is important for the teacher to be enthusiastic and to motivate students to work more actively in exploring and analysing topics in the new subject. But previous lack of knowledge can be a real problem and can lead to student passivity in 16–19 classes. In such cases, the theory can go down very badly. The leap between GCSE and A level is very difficult and you can feel ill-equipped in terms of use of terminology. Students in such a class might think little work would be required. How wrong they will discover they are!

Many existing teachers have been educated predominantly in degrees which do not match A level specifications. As such, some do not automatically possess the requisite subject knowledge to teach A level with confidence. They are essentially operating as non-specialists and the danger of this is they can resort to employing traditional teacher-directed methods, and to be less innovative and dynamic in their teaching than they otherwise would, resorting to lectures, timed essays and going over essays.

Of course exam training and practice for timed essays is important. However, a cycle of ineffective A level teaching might continue unchecked unless PGCE courses, and school or college mentors take on the issue of new subjects. Where are effective teachers of these subjects to be found with both subject knowledge and pedagogic skills? How will they then contribute to the training of new teachers of A level?

There can be a clear split between the experience of those trainees who themselves have a relevant degree, and those with a degree not matching the A level subject-knowledge requirements. Even for those who do, significant personal effort has to be made (wider reading) to update that subject knowledge to match the requirements of A level teaching.

Conversely, some inexperienced teachers might receive a confidence boost by being welcomed as a 16–19 subject specialist with relevant expertise, and thus be encouraged to do their own thing and play on the strengths of their subject knowledge. However, being given this kind of free rein has its down side. Such trainees are essentially pitched into 16–19 teaching on their own, operating outside any framework of training and support that should be in place. Are they likely to develop an effective repertoire of 16–19 teaching skills independently?

ITT MENTORS AND SUBJECT KNOWLEDGE

What position can mentors adopt in debates over subject knowledge with trainee teachers? Are tensions about the content and purpose of 16–19 subjects made explicit? Issues might include:

- What is the appropriate canon for post-16 students?
- What competing standpoints are battling for control of your A level subject?
- How does 16–19 subject knowledge impact on effective 16–19 teaching?
- How can subject knowledge be differentiated post-16?
- How can teachers take account of students' cultural capital and the level of challenge presented to them in KS4?
- Do beliefs about subject knowledge cause a clash between didactic traditions post-16 and a desire to value learner autonomy?

A trainee's view of what is valuable in 16–19 will influence their choice of strategies when planning teaching. As such, mentor involvement is vital in training so that the two come together in effective synergy. Drake and Dart (1994) for example, have reported mentor awareness of the discrepancy between literature-based English degrees and the secondary English curriculum. One simple mentor task in this context is in text selection: which books will Year 12s be studying when the trainee teacher comes in?

This is an obvious but important point. A poorly chosen text (usually an over-ambitious choice given the range of students in the class) can lead to problems with differentiation and tensions in relation to lack of cultural capital. PGCE students are under great pressure during periods of teaching practice. NQTs are under great pressure to cope with a demanding timetable. Teaching at 16–19 adds to that pressure, requiring intensive preparation and heavy marking and often attracting little feedback in terms of student response. This pressure is exacerbated if the choice of text is problematic and the trainee can feel thrown in at the deep end.

This sort of pressure on trainee teachers is made even worse if mentor support is unforthcoming, as poor or inappropriate text selection can also lead to a fall back to traditional, transmission models of teaching. Daw (1996) noted that successful departments chose syllabuses and texts appropriate to their pupils' needs.

But if trainee teachers are forced into adopting a more traditional approach to their 16–19 teaching as a deficit model (as, for example in 'my Year 12 students don't know anything about x, so I have to lecture') the result is to deny 16–19 students a range of learning opportunities. The result may be that it is the weaker students who will suffer.

The situation is compounded if trainees emulate existing traditional practice as observed in their partner school (described in Macfarlane 1993, Rainbow 1993). They are then unable to practise the skills they will need as NQTs and beyond.

Conversations with mentors suggest that one of the keys to effective 16–19 teaching is getting pupils to think, and not to spoon-feed them. They have to be taught how to prioritise material, to analyse rather than simply describe. In many subjects they need quite sophisticated essay-writing skills that they have not come across before. That's very difficult to teach them. A lot of new teachers to A level just concentrate on going through a topic, without teaching them these thinking skills. Trainee teachers often can't see the wood for the trees. They perhaps get bogged down, not realising that it takes Year 12 pupils a good year before they start to develop these skills. Crucially, the weaker ones don't acquire them without being taught.

It is hard to find evidence of mentors presenting this depth of insight into the problems of 16–19 teaching to their trainees. This unwillingness to intervene might confirm Davies's (1993) description of mentors failing to connect subject ideology and classroom practice in English. The extreme example would be the trainee who, after her final teaching practice, queried:

> How do you fill two-hour lessons with a range of constructive activities to keep A level pupils engaged?

This sort of observation is worrying. The trainee had completed the required period of placement in two schools, seemingly without observing, or experiencing herself, a well-planned and well executed 16–19 lesson. She could start teaching as an NQT with no confidence in the strategies likely to work effectively to develop learning in the 16–19 classroom. The effect on her own professional self-image, and the 16–19 students she will teach, could be profoundly negative. The professional image of 16–19 teachers is closely bound up with deeply held beliefs about subject knowledge, and this student had that knocked by her experience of learning (or in her case not learning) to teach 16–19. If repeated in other contexts, this is unlikely to help teacher retention and is unlikely to aid the improvement of 16–19 standards.

It is easy to understand why mentors might keep out of the 16–19 classroom during training. There are many other pressures on their time, and 16–19 teaching can appear less 'risky', less likely to need mentor intervention, compared to the kind of support envisaged for 11–16 classroom management. Many mentors are therefore unable to provide a range of challenging opportunities at 16–19. It is a shame that few appeared to explicitly recognise the potential benefits of trainees bringing new or experimental approaches to 16–19 learning. The following mentor's reflection is an exception:

> I like taking postgraduate students. . . . They come with fresh ideas, new ways of getting into texts and experimental ways of looking at things. . . . Our student initially planned a post-16 lesson in the IT room with the internet . . . none of

us do that at the moment so we're delighted that she is going to show us a way forward here.

A fuller and more explicit agenda for 16–19 training in ITT is urgently needed. One could be created from the following comment:

> A lot does depend on your specific subject knowledge and knowing your group and trying a variety of strategies. . . . useful would be ideas on how to approach things at the outset . . . how to actually introduce pupils fresh from Year 11 to the whole of A level work.
>
> (PGCE trainee)

SUBJECT-KNOWLEDGE CULTURES: THE PRESSURE TO ADAPT

Arthur *et al.* (1997) report on the importance of departmental cultures for ITT students on placement. The prevailing ethos of 16–19 teaching can be a powerful one and many trainees seek to adapt their view of 16–19 teaching to that of the department in which they train.

> They are fairly traditional in their approach here, so I found it quite easy coming and picking up what they do. . . . I observed one sixth-form lesson and it was exactly like I would go about it.
>
> (PGCE trainee)

In my visit to this placement, I observed a Year 12 lesson in which the trainee was quite happy to fit in with the norms of that department. However, there can be problems with this approach, particularly if the trainee feels constrained by the 16–19 context in which they are working.

> Just because one teacher teaches successfully in a certain way post-16 that certainly is not the only way. . . . If you copy one person with a particular style because it works for them that doesn't guarantee it's going to work for you . . . that could be quite difficult for trainees.
>
> (Mentor)

However, trainees can be less than clear on how they should be developing their own views of the subject in relation to their mentors:

> I found the utilisation of contextual knowledge on an historical/biographical basis was acceptable for one teacher but not the other . . . this reflected the personal

approaches of the teacher. . . . I felt I had a lot to offer in this area from my degree, but was quickly 'kicked into touch' by my mentor.

(PGCE trainee)

Tension in the micropolitics of a subject department can affect how inexperienced teachers use their own subject knowledge. Often, trainees work alongside, and are observed by subject teachers other than their mentor. Thus, for consistency, feedback should be framed in terms of the Standards, and should be supported with what Goodwyn (1997) calls 'accurate empathy'.

CONCLUSION

She hasn't taught a full text at A level . . . in that sense she's ill-prepared isn't she? Post-16 I think I am falling down in that I haven't discussed the syllabus enough with her . . . at a much earlier stage we need to get examples of A level work.

(Mentor)

Teaching at 16–19 can be a frustrating experience for many trainees. The experience of mentoring in ITT can be hands-off or unchallenging in the 16–19 classroom. This becomes a particular problem for trainees struggling to develop differentiated approaches to subject knowledge (for example Year 12 students traumatised by the leap from Year 11 GCSE work). It is also a problem for trainees offered practice in subjects outside the expertise of mainstream teachers in the school or college without the modelling of effective practice.

Lively discussion about subject knowledge in school and college departments, aiming to cross-fertilise teaching strategies across classes, would contribute to more effective 16–19 teaching. Would such discussions about subject knowledge in your own discipline be effective?

SUBJECT ASSOCIATIONS

- NATE (National Association for the Teaching of English): www.nate.org.uk
- ASE (Association for Science Education): www.ase.org.uk
- Geographical Association: www.geography.org.uk
- Historical Association: www.history.org.uk
- Association for Language Learning: www.languagelearn.co.uk
- CILT (Centre for Information on Language Teaching and Research): www.cilt.org.uk
- NSEAD (National Association for Education in Art and Design): www.nsead.org

- The Association for ICT in Education: www.acitt.org.uk
- The Association for the Teaching of the Social Sciences: www.le.ac.uk/education/centres/ATSS
- The Association of Teachers of Mathematics: www.atm.org.uk
- The Mathematical Association: www.m-a.org.uk
- The Economics and Business Education Association: www.ebea.org.uk
- The Physical Education Association in the United Kingdom: http://tele-school.org.uk/pea/
- The Music Education Council: www.mec.org.uk/

HEADLINES

Subject knowledge is essential to effective 16–19 teaching:

- Confident teaching comes from subject expertise.
- Subject mastery for 16–19 teaching does not automatically relate to degree-level knowledge.
- Subject knowledge is not static. Work with a mentor and departmental colleagues to develop and sustain good subject knowledge.

6   Assessment 16–19

Qualifying to Teach Standards

3.1.2   *Use teaching and learning objectives to plan lessons, and sequences of lessons, showing how they will assess pupils' learning. . . . Take account of and support pupils' varying needs so that girls and boys, from all ethnic groups, can make good progress.*

3.2.1   *They make appropriate use of a range of monitoring and assessment strategies to evaluate pupils' progress towards planned learning objectives, and use this information to improve their own planning and teaching.*

3.2.2   *They monitor and assess as they teach, giving immediate and constructive feedback to support pupils as they learn. They involve pupils in reflecting on, evaluating and improving their own performance.*

3.2.3   *They are able to assess pupils' progress accurately using, as relevant . . . criteria from national qualifications, the requirements of awarding bodies. . . . They may have guidance from an experienced teacher where appropriate.*

OBJECTIVES

Reading this chapter and engaging actively with the tasks will enable you to:

- reflect on the different uses of assessment in 16–19 education
- consider how to make best use of formative feedback
- understand A level and AVCE grading
- implement teaching strategies which will produce evidence to meet QTS Standards 3.1.2, 3.2.1–3.2.7, and FENTO Standards F1–2.

3.2.4   They identify and support more able pupils, those who are working below age-related expectations, those who are failing to achieve their potential in learning, and those who experience behavioural, emotional and social difficulties. They may have guidance from an experienced teacher where appropriate.

3.2.5   With the help of an experienced teacher, they can identify the levels of attainment of pupils learning English as an additional language. They begin to analyse the language demands and learning activities in order to provide cognitive challenge as well as language support.

3.2.6   They record pupils' progress and achievements systematically to provide evidence of the range of their work, progress and attainment over time. They use this to help pupils review their own progress and to inform planning.

3.2.7   They are able to use records as a basis for reporting on pupils' attainment and progress orally and in writing, concisely, informatively and accurately for parents, carers, other professionals and pupils.

FENTO Standards
F   *Assessing the outcomes of learning and learners' achievements*
 F1   *use appropriate assessment methods to measure learning achievement*
 F2   *make use of assessment information*

ASSESSMENT IMPERATIVES

> At post-16 the pressure seems to be so focused on passing exams and getting through texts that the teaching approaches at both schools appeared to be rather stifled, they spoon-fed pupils. . . . Whilst I recognise the pressure of work, I question whether a more challenging approach isn't more effective: certainly I have been surprised by what students can do if pushed and what little they will do if allowed to.
>
> (Trainee teacher)

Students at 16–19 have chosen to be in education, and have opted for (or been selected for) a course of study in which the final assessment is crucial to their progression to HE, employment or training. However, this summative assessment, usually publicly certificated, is only one part of effective assessment 16–19. For example, 16–19 students ought to have had their strengths and learning needs assessed at the start of Year 12 as part of a thorough diagnostic assessment. Teachers need to be aware of the significance of this, alongside ALIS data and the relevant GCSE score in their subject. And as the students journey through their chosen course, an ongoing and dynamic review of what has been learnt should form a regular part of their formative assessment.

Assessment thus impinges on every aspect of 16–19 teaching, as it is a key ongoing indicator and final judgement (however flawed) of how effective a learner individual students have been. It is therefore important that 16–19 teachers are themselves skilled in the ways of assessment. No student should reach the end of their course without having being assessed in a way that informs clearly their own aspirations.

Ofsted have taken a particular interest in this. For example, in science (Ofsted 2001p), inspectors favour:

- clear assessment schemes, which students themselves understand
- assessed work returned to students which is carefully annotated with corrections and identified omissions
- record keeping which is intended to monitor progress
- targets focused on specific learning goals (individual and group) which meet AS or A2 assessment objectives as appropriate
- specific revision needs analysed.

This is a major undertaking for any teacher, and is certainly daunting for an inexperienced or trainee teacher new to 16–19. It indicates that assessment cannot be taken lightly. Assessment should not be bolted-on as an afterthought, and needs to be incorporated into planning and integrated into teaching strategies.

So given that all 16–19 teachers need to be effective assessors of student work, and would aim to assess as professionally and effectively as they can, where to start? One way is to spend some time reflecting on your own experience of being assessed, particularly in your own experience of 16–19 education.

Task 22

Did you take A levels, or a vocational course? Did you have to retake an O level or GCSE? Do you remember how it felt? Is it the outcome you recall most clearly (success or failure as measured by a grade in an examination)? Or is it the process you recall, the months of revision with no clear idea of what you were revising for? The stress of entering the examination room, the empty feeling when the question paper was not what you had hoped for, or the delight when you saw something you were expecting and had prepared for? Looking back, did you ever misunderstand what was required of you? Do you regret a lack of feedback?

It is really vital that we are aware of the power and significance of assessment for our 16–19 students. Do not repeat with your students any of the assessment disappointments you may have experienced. Given the increasing number of commentators and practitioners who have bemoaned the dominance of assessment in 16–19 education recently, it is important we try to set only those assessment tasks which are appropriate. Guard against assessing automatically, for the sake of it. There is a grave danger that we are over-assessing students rather than enabling them to learn, so ask yourself what you want the assessment to reveal.

Of course you should be using assessment to check learning. But be clear why you are using it. Is it as a course requirement (for example, submission of coursework to an Awarding Body in a form prescribed by them)? Is it an institutional requirement (for example an internal grading with a parents' evening coming up, the form of which you have some control over)? Or is it a part of your ongoing formative support for 16–19 learners to help in target setting and the meeting of targets? Whichever is the case, there should be a detailed marking scheme your students have seen and understood.

A key imperative is that 16–19 teachers keep effective records of student progress. Institutions may have different approaches to doing this, but this is one area where the impact of ICT makes record keeping easier and more accessible. Be clear on expectations in your department, and share data with a colleague who teaches the same group as you.

VARIETIES OF 16–19 ASSESSMENT

Of course assessment can take many forms. For the kind of formal, written examination paper still used in A level, a product that might be a single answer is sent off to be externally marked. Such assessment will compare the performance of students across a large cohort. It is likely to be criterion-referenced, measured against a pre-determined standard in which the criteria are open. For this sort of assessment you have very little choice as the teacher. Often, all you can do is rehearse as much as possible with the students, with feedback aimed at them entering the examination hall being absolutely clear what to expect, and confident in how to achieve their best.

In other forms of assessment, as the teacher you can control what is going on far more. You might be able to negotiate, you will certainly be able to mediate for your students. Such examples might take the form of a piece of continuous assessment, or a piece of coursework in which formative assessment is intended to support learning. There might also be the possibility of a unique assessment opportunity, like the informal teacher observation of an internal process (perhaps an open-ended, creative task).

There are of course a number of issues affecting assessment at 16–19. The following are significant for inexperienced teachers (see Armitage *et al.* 2003):

- Because 16–19 teachers are acutely conscious of time pressures, they can be wary of any assessment that looks elaborate, like role play or decision-making simulation. Hence there is a tendency to fall back on tried and trusted (and traditional) assessment tasks like essays or report writing. Even these offer a wide range of assessment possibilities if used creatively. Do you want students to discuss, to analyse, to evaluate, to compare, to contrast? Are your students even clear what you mean by these? Try not to neglect the possibility of assessing slightly more adventurously (for example through oral group presentations, small-scale research in which students are assessed both for the collection and analysis of data, or portfolios supporting a video production).

- Some 16–19 teachers may doubt the capacity of students to assess their own peers. They fear that students have neither the skills, the understanding nor the inclination to assess one another's work. This is unfortunate, is probably untrue and represents a missed opportunity to engage students fully in the process of assessment. If you have a chance to try it, it is likely to be a real eye-opener, particularly for the students who will experience the potency of discussing what is good and what is not so good (and why). The insights into their own performance can be immense. Ofsted has reported (2001a) that in the most effective Drama assessment practice, teachers deliberately nurtured peer assessment and self-assessment skills. They often achieved this by sharing models of good performance with students, alongside the marking criteria. Skills checklists were used by teachers and students as they watched practical work, and were linked to target setting. Is there anything similar you could do in your 16–19 teaching?

- Do 16–19 teachers always have access to the resources they need to assess efficiently? For example, are there video and audio cassettes for use in moderating oral presentations? Are there sufficient CD Roms and floppy disks available for all students to practise powerpoint presentations? Can assessed practicals be carried out in existing labs? Are there the resources to mount an exhibition, or to present an arts performance to the public? In these latter cases, if you are able to enthuse your students with an explicit understanding of the criteria they are to be assessed against, they may 'take over' and run the assessment as an experiential learning event. This can be particularly effective if you are fortunate enough to teach on the few remaining BTEC National courses, but can be adopted for A level and AVCE.

- Are 16–19 teachers over-anxious about encouraging students to make use of logs or diaries in which to record subjective judgements about their work? These can be a useful adjunct to project work, but need to be checked regularly, and students need to realise how such 'field notes' can be drawn on as an aspect of assessed work.

- Are 16–19 teachers overly troubled by differentiation in assessment? How flexible or comfortable are we in managing assessment rather than letting it manage our teaching? Can we not introduce alternative tasks and questions within a given assessment, such as oral rather than the ubiquitous written responses? Can we try out an ethnically relevant comprehension, or a numeracy paper in a student's first language? Do objective tests like multiple choice, or true/false quizzes, or 'fill in the space' worksheets help meet the needs of the broad range of learners?

Teacher assessment at 16–19 is likely to be far more effective if it is integrated into a system of reviewing, recording and reporting achievement. This is placing the student at the heart of the assessment process, enhancing the likelihood that students will fully understand the comments and grading on their work. No student is going to learn from feedback that is merely judgemental, or is phrased in such vague terms as to be worse than useless. Ipsative assessment, in which performance is graded against previous achievement, can be especially important in target setting.

EFFECTIVE FEEDBACK

The feedback you supply on any piece of assessed work should be supporting that student's learning. So it is imperative you think carefully about the form that feedback will take. It is also important to consider how you will take action in relation to individual students who may require particular attention.

Effective feedback can be characterised by:

- clear and directly stated reasons for a grade (or a tick)
- constructive and relevant advice
- helpful attitude in the tone, inviting student evaluation and dialogue
- specific rather than vague description of room for improvement next time
- good timing (for advice to impact on the next piece of assessed work).

This should not be done in isolation. Do 16–19 teachers make enough of Examiners' reports and mark schemes with their students? Are students always made familiar with the assessment objectives as spelt out in the subject criteria, and repeated in each published specification? In your subject, for example, it is worth checking if objectives for A2 modules are different from AS modules, indicating progression. If so, are teachers explicit about this with their students? Are students always appropriately prepared for being assessed in the synoptic modules when assessment objectives are tested together?

These are critical considerations. In English A level for example, students' conceptual understanding has to be evaluated, together with the clarity of their analytical thinking about language. Assessment cannot be nebulous in relation to such challenges. Too often, 16–19 students do not know what criteria they are being assessed against, and do not know why they have been given a particular grade. Rigour, even in 'difficult' areas of assessment, has to be seen in action and 16–19 teachers have to be on top of such demands. We should also ensure that, if extensive formative feedback has been given, students know how to interpret it, have opportunities to reflect upon it and can utilise it in a structured way for the benefit of their next piece of work.

Assessing project work at 16–19 can present particular problems for both students and teachers. One way round this is to exemplify previous good projects, and discuss how those examples meet the criteria for grades. Both you and your students will want to know what a lower ability project will need to do to pass, while with the high attaining project all students will need to be clear what it would have to do to get a top grade.

One drawback in 16–19 assessment is that opportunities for student plagiarism have become far more prevalent since the internet became really accessible. These can be minimised by teacher planning. For project work, try building up an archive of copies of previous contents pages, aims and bibliographies. This can provide students with a starting point and the likelihood that their subsequent focus will be sharper. Project work offers assessment opportunities for students who might not otherwise shine, but teacher planning has to be effective. Is there an accessible collection of 'techniques' books? Is there good access to IT for the students to work on their own? Is there a collection of cuttings files and document boxes kept up to date by the library?

Students will need to be absolutely clear about the required length and the assessment criteria of projects, because they are required to demonstrate skills of independent learning. Some students will shine at this, and structure their own work automatically. Others will need more support to manage such a task to an effective and appropriate outcome. The effective 16–19 teacher will build their own milestones into any monitoring. Such deadlines should be treated as such, particularly for those students whose organisational skills do not match their ambition.

It is also worth considering how you will support students formatively during their project work. Some students can be very demanding of your time, while others will not take advantage of the support they are entitled to. Good advice comes from Turton (1996) who suggests that teachers draw up an appointments schedule for individual consultations, and issue three tokens per student, entitling them to 30 minutes of one-to-one advice and guidance. He also suggests that students should tape record the sessions rather than laboriously taking notes (and inevitably missing the key idea). This will make the ongoing assessment of project work more manageable, and the support sessions more productive.

When it comes to assessing completed or partially completed projects, it is always a good idea to mark with another (more experienced) teacher, and to allow the students opportunities to receive feedback on drafts. It is also worth checking student plans in draft, any notes they have made and annotations they have made to texts. Sometimes it can be more effective to use a marking sheet, extended feedback form or pro-forma rather than 'bleed' all over a script (Ofsted 2001a, Le Versha and Nicholls 2003). This can contribute to higher quality feedback on fewer examples, rather than cursory comments on more occasions. In the end, 16–19 teachers have to recognise the implications of the critical role they have in managing student projects.

Formative assessment is thus critical for effective 16–19 teaching. Teachers are becoming far more used to setting targets for their students, but target setting has to be integrated into ongoing teaching. For this to be effective, the targets need to be 'SMART' ones.

Task 23

It is worth checking the last time you set targets for a student to see if they were:

- Specific
- Measurable
- Achievable
- Relevant
- Time-bound

It is also worth checking carefully to clarify the kind of mark scheme used in your Awarding Body's subject specifications. Is it banded with level descriptors, or does it give set marks for can do/can't do answers? Such insight will inform the targets given to students and the approach you take to preparing students for terminal assessments.

It is also important that any assessment you devise is transparent. Do not be afraid to provide students with very clear guidance of what they are being expected to do. It should also be fair, in that all students should be able to complete it, but it should challenge the higher achieving students to develop further. It is also important you are clear whether you are testing them (essentially a piece of summative feedback) or whether you are seeking to develop them (a piece of formative feedback).

Subject-specific examples of effective 16–19 assessment practice tell a similar but significant story. In Music Ofsted suggests (2001n) for practical and compositional assignments, students must be clear how they are being assessed. Essentially, this means checking that they understand what they are required to do in order to do well. In Dance (Ofsted 2002a) 16–19 teachers are reminded to comment and respond in student notebooks and files. They should also correct students' technical and performance errors as necessary, and should relate theory to practice in any assessment. And in Art and Design (Ofsted 2001b) 16–19 teachers are expected to prepare students to make and take constructive criticism. This should be done in the context of teacher targets which are relevant, but not unreasonably challenging. Inspection reports are critical if targets from performance monitoring are insufficiently focused on learning goals. It is the responsibility of the teacher to be clear about project briefs and deadlines, and the staging points along the way. They are also encouraged to utilise as far as possible 'live' assignments and competition briefs.

In Psychology, (Ofsted 2002b) 16–19 teachers are encouraged to get students to assess their own performance, having been given the marking criteria. Teachers are also considered effective if they praise good attenders and chase non-attenders.

A reminder about poor assessment practice can be a stimulating prompt towards greater effectiveness. In Business Education, Ofsted (2001c) criticises the infrequent marking of student work. This can of course mean students have not been able to develop their understanding and skills from teacher feedback in one assignment before the next one is due. It also means students can become cynical about the amount of effort to be expended on assignments. They might feel that their 16–19 teacher does not care, or as is more likely, that they have been unable to manage their time to assess efficiently. Poor turnaround can certainly reduce student motivation and contribute to insufficient progress being made.

In Science, Ofsted (2001p) is critical of marking which is not as thorough as it might be, with basic errors missed. This points to a need for a clear departmental policy on expectations about 16–19 assessment and scheduling, with some support given to new and inexperienced 16–19 teachers being provided.

In PE, Ofsted (2001o) suggests that the most helpful assessment draws on practice across the whole range of the syllabus. This is particularly important in those subjects where different teachers (perhaps based in different parts of the institution) specialise in teaching different areas of the syllabus. Some, for example, will always wish to teach the project component, or will always see themselves as leading on practical work, while others will feel they 'own' specific essay-centred papers. Unfortunately, the design of AS and A2 modules can force departments to organise their teaching in this way. The result can be a somewhat odd experience for students, as they are assessed in discrete units, and teachers do not always make connections with learning in other parts of the subject specifications.

16–19 MARKING SCALES

For A level, it is important for new teachers to consider the impact of the proportion of internally assessed coursework to the final grade, and the effect this might have on their own assessment practice. Normally, this will be a maximum of 30% although some practically orientated or creative subjects will have a higher proportion. The contrast with AVCEs is interesting, because the normal proportion of coursework on these is more likely to be 70 per cent. Thus teachers on AVCE programmes have a potentially greater role in recommending the final grade awarded. There is also a big difference in how teachers prepare candidates, depending on the kind of assessment.

Of course, all internally assessed work at A level or AVCE is moderated, either by a postal sample to a moderator, or by a visit to an institution from a moderator. In either case, the moderator's role is to confirm (or adjust) rank orderings according to pre-set boundaries based on criteria from the Awarding Body.

An AS is awarded on a total of 300 marks (not necessarily weighted equally across the three units). This equates to 50 per cent of the final, full A level, if the student goes on to take three new units at A2 (worth 300 more marks). The total thus possible for an A level is 600 marks, on a Uniform Mark Scale (UMS). Each unit's UMS mark is added together to give a final grade. So the boundaries for an individual AS unit are minimum marks of:

A: 80
B: 70
C: 60
D: 50
E: 40

The full three-unit AS is awarded on the following minimum marks:

A: 240
B: 210
C: 180
D: 150
E: 120

The A level or six-unit AVCE is awarded on minimum marks of:

A: 480
B: 420
C: 360
D: 300
E: 240

Anything which does not meet the minimum mark for a grade E will be given a U (unclassified) grade.

This information can be seen on a student's statement of results. It is important that individual 16–19 teachers, as well as department heads, monitor disparities in assessment across different units. This can be an important indicator of where support needs to be given if overall results are to improve.

For many students in 16–19 education, the grades gained from A level or AVCEs will be of crucial significance in accessing opportunities for higher education. All institutions offering HE in the UK will make offers and grant places to students based on an agreed UCAS tariff. This will cover pass grades at A level, AS, AVCE dual awards, single units and Key Skills units.

The UCAS grade tariff for AS is:

E: 20
D: 30
C: 40
B: 50
A: 60

For A level it is:

E: 40
D: 60
C: 80
B: 100
A: 120

For a double-award (12–unit) AVCE it is:

E: 80
D: 120
C: 160
B: 200
A: 240

There are also points for passing single units, from 7 for an E grade up to 20 for an A grade. In addition, points are awarded for the three main Key Skill units, depending on the skill level. For example, Level 3 communication, which indicates achievement supporting work at A level, brings 20 points.

What this means in reality is that an offer from a new university for a degree place in a science/engineering discipline, might attract a 210 point offer, which could mean a student needing to gain a grade C and a grade D in two A levels, and a grade C and a grade D in two AS levels. A student applying for Law or Medicine at a Russell-group university might get a three A, or 360 point offer.

CONCLUSION

Assessment is hard. The challenge for 16–19 teachers is to make assessment practices an integrated part of their planned teaching strategy, and not to allow their approach to teaching to be dictated by assessment demands. To be effective, assessment must support and develop student learning. Making assessment criteria transparent to students, and drawing on the widest range of approaches to assessment tasks, can enable 16–19 teachers to tame the assessment demon.

To do this, assessment must be seen as a process, which teachers engage in during the whole of 16–19 education to:

- diagnose initial learning needs
- test understanding of content
- develop appropriate writing or practical skills
- prepare for summative AS/A2 or AVCE examinations.

This is a process best done collaboratively. For trainees or NQTs, this is most effectively done with a mentor. For more experienced teachers, moderation of assessment approaches and judgements with a colleague is far more effective than struggling on your own. It is always worth sharing a couple of essays from one another's piles, or observing a couple of oral presentations from one another's groups. If necessary, your colleague's students can form an audience for your class.

Ofsted is particularly interested in comparative data on assessment. For example, is there evidence that male and female students perform differently in the same subject, or across different subjects or courses. Do ethnic minority or bilingual students perform differently? Are results at A level, AS or AVCE better or worse than expected from GCSE results? As an individual teacher in the 16–19 classroom, it is worth analysing your own classes' data and discussing the significance of disparities with colleagues. Where there are concerns, it is important to investigate reasons, and to develop a plan to address that in your teaching.

HEADLINES

- Manage 16–19 assessment, do not let it manage your teaching.
- Try to remember what it felt like to be assessed as a 16–19 student.
- Concentrate on clear, full, formative feedback to 16–19 students.
- Understand UMS and UCAS points. Check students' previous attainment against these.

7   Active learning in the 16–19 classroom

Qualifying to Teach Standards

2.5   *Know how to use ICT effectively, both to teach their subject and to support their wider professional role.*

2.7   *Know a range of strategies to promote good behaviour and establish a purposeful teaching environment.*

3.3.3   *They teach clearly structured lessons or sequences of work which interest and motivate pupils and which:*

    – make learning objectives clear to pupils

    – employ interactive teaching methods and collaborative group work

    – promote active and independent learning that enables pupils to think for themselves, and to plan and manage their own learning.

3.3.6   *They take account of the varying interests, experiences and achievements of boys and girls, and pupils from different cultural and ethnic groups, to help pupils make good progress.*

OBJECTIVES

Reading this chapter and engaging actively with the tasks will enable you to:

- reflect on the need for active learning in the 16–19 classroom
- consider how to prevent behavioural issues affecting 16–19 teaching
- embrace the opportunities ICT provides to support effective 16–19 teaching
- implement teaching strategies which will produce evidence to meet QTS Standards 2.5, 2.7, 3.3.3, 3.3.6, 3.3.9, 3.3.10, and FENTO Standards C1–3.

3.3.9   They set high expectations for pupil behaviour and establish a clear framework for classroom discipline to anticipate and manage pupils' behaviour constructively, and promote self-control and independence.

3.3.10   They use ICT effectively in their teaching.

FENTO Standards

C   Developing and using a range of teaching and learning techniques

   C1   promote and encourage individual learning

   C2   facilitate learning in groups

   C3   facilitate learning through experience

WHAT DO 16–19 LEARNERS NEED?

One theme running through this book, and to some extent providing a rationale for it, is that the 16–19 teacher is working with an increasingly wide range of learners. Early research findings into the impact of Curriculum 2000 on teaching and learning (Hodgson and Spours 2003) suggest that, because of this, whole-class teaching can appear the only option in the 16–19 classroom. But each individual student in the class must be engaged in the 16–19 experience. This is more likely to be effective if the teacher sees themselves as a facilitator of learning, someone who sets out with the aim of guiding, stimulating and prompting all students.

Inexperienced 16–19 teachers can assume a break in learning styles at 16, as if the completion of compulsory education has automatically produced students capable of effective independent learning. This goes against what most generic learning theories say about learning styles, and 16–19 teachers need to recognise that particular approaches, particular learning activities and particular materials need to be utilised. This requires an active approach to 16–19 learning, which to be effective needs to transcend the limitations of teacher-directed whole-class teaching. It involves you in carefully planned use of discussion, peer and group collaboration and student 'ownership' of learning tasks.

For active learning to be effective, planning and organisation is crucial. It requires a meticulous consideration of how you can structure opportunity for individual work against pair, group or whole-class work. However, it should not appear over-complex. The key is to facilitate student responsibility for their own learning, both by active engagement in lesson tasks, and by deliberate skills development. Student confidence is crucial, and you can develop it through carefully prepared group work. If the 16–19 teacher is front-loading and spoon-feeding all of the time, learner confidence will not be enhanced.

As an inexperienced 16–19 teacher, you may find yourself being a relentless (and often unconscious) director of learning in the classroom, because you are more likely to be prone to misconceptions about your students. Teachers inexperienced in 16–19 teaching are often driven by an understandable desire to get through the content (lots of it) against a strict and unforgiving assessment deadline. You should realise that this is rarely a successful way to enable deep learning. Although the introduction of active learning strategies does not, in itself, guarantee effective learning, as Ofsted reports (2001a), it is the pace of learning, rather than the pace of specific activities, that is the key to effective 16–19 teaching. If you can introduce active learning strategies, giving students the time to reflect, to think and to puzzle, students are more likely to be fully engaged.

You can further 16–19 learning by extending beyond a reliance on teacher-led presentation, however tempting that may be, given all the constraints in Year 12. By carefully planned interactions, by activities which enable learners to discover for themselves, and by evaluations which feature mini-tests and quizzes, you can forge a positive and engaged learning environment.

Teacher encounters with 16–19 students are usually intuitive and automatic despite the intensity of the learning relationships in the classroom. As teachers, we do not always have enough time to stop and think about the effectiveness of what we are doing. So, one step towards active learning is if you start listening to 16–19 learners. By listening carefully to what our students say to us, it can be possible to make our teaching more experimental and active. We should note responses when we present new ideas, when we discuss and probe using open questions to draw out students' understanding. Teachers can start to support learning by the responses they make to questioning. A colleague's observational feedback on your questioning and presentation techniques can be extremely useful in helping to develop confidence in active learning techniques with 16–19 year olds.

Questioning is an important and somewhat neglected skill. A tendency is for 16–19 teachers to engage in a kind of teacher-led quiz, but this can easily degenerate into something dominated by a few, more orally confident students. It is certainly not an effective way of engaging a whole class. It is also unfortunate that most classroom questions are not especially challenging, and do not prompt thought-provoking or intriguing reflection. Part of the problem is that 16–19 teachers tend not to wait very long for answers in such sessions, and tend to wait even less for answers from lower ability or passive students.

Good practice in any 16–19 class is to endeavour to include all students by directing questions differentiated according to ability. It is worth reflecting by self-monitoring (or getting an observer to comment on) whether more of your questions are directed at student x or group y, or whether questions are asked to a particular student.

While closed questions can be effective at the start of sessions to recap and check learning (for example, in Government and Politics, how many constituencies are there in the UK?), it is important for teachers to move on to more open questioning which will provoke discussion, lead to higher level thought and exploration of cause and effect (for example, in Communication Studies, give me a reason why it might be argued language use is directly related to social class?). The questions should be framed during planning, to enable consideration to be given to vocabulary and to whom they will be addressed. That way, the spontaneous 'false' open question, the answer to which is already known, or which adds nothing to the content of the lesson, can be avoided. Authentic open questions can then lead into the exploration of more speculative ideas.

GROUP WORKING 16–19

Sometimes, inexperienced teachers can launch straight into a surfeit of small group work with 16–19 students. They assume students are all equally motivated, subject-focused and capable of working independently of the teacher. This does not always produce the intended outcome, and indeed students can be uncomfortable with such an approach imposed upon them. It can even be counter-productive, setting up opportunities for individual students to dominate, for some students to remain completely disengaged, and for immature behaviour to develop.

In such circumstances, have you considered how well the 16–19 students are likely to work together in groups? It is crucial to consider whether all students have worked this way before. Some may well have come from institutions, and from subjects, in which effective group work was the norm in GCSE classes. However, others may be far more used to teacher-directed tasks and teacher exposition, and simply not have the experience of learning in this way. Even if you can establish with confidence the experience students have previously had of working in groups, do you know for how long your students have enjoyed this way of working?

To be fully effective, the prior group-learning experience needs to have been co-operative and participative. If it has not, you may need to structure some supported activities which will demonstrate how that might be achieved. Some ice-breaking activities and problem-solving activities can focus students on the positive experience that effective group learning can produce. You should initially set up the groups with specified roles (chair, secretary, timekeeper) and you should encourage them to move furniture so that group discussion can occur naturally. You might wish to allow groups to self-select, but that can lead to students being isolated or in gender or peer cliques. It is easy to number students 1–4 around the class, and organise them in that way.

You can set up discussion groups with specific questions on a topic or piece of text. 'Expert' groups can each be given a different topic to present to the other groups, or to respond as a kind of brains trust. Other groupings can present different sides of an argument or brainstorm ideas in an open way. But all require you to provide clear instructions at the start, and need you to circulate and involve yourself as necessary. The key to successful group work is to keep all students on task, to keep all tasks to time and to ensure all students are involved. It is also important to carefully manage the feedback, whether you ask for it to be delivered orally by a nominee, by the group, or accompanied by a powerpoint presentation. Students can be hugely disappointed in activities like this if you inadvertently allow the session to run out of time.

One real danger for younger teachers is the notion of students responding to what can look like 'trendy teacher' syndrome. This can be difficult, as 16–19 students are sensitive to what they are asked to do in classrooms, and any suggestion of ill-considered, narcissistic or ego-inflating strategies could turn them against you. So, the key to engaging students fully in group working is to take the students with you by a clear and explicit justification of the intended teaching method. This of course requires you to be flexible, and experimental too.

Some group behaviour in 16–19 classrooms can be mercurial and unpredictable. Yet you must aim for the groups to offer a supportive environment for learning. For the effective teacher, the notion of getting classes to work in groups should be that the groups take on a life of their own, and move beyond mere teaching groups. Ideally, when engaging in group work, the learning emerging across the whole class should be more than the sum of its parts.

Students cannot, particularly at the start of Year 12, be left to their own devices in a group, to 'get on with' whatever task you have set them. You need to be a genuine facilitator, setting the agenda and providing regular feedback as you circulate and keep groups reminded of the time remaining. Crucial to effective group work is that you keep a very close eye on the time, and on the progress groups are making on-task, so that plenary feedback can be shared, supported and commented on without being rushed or omitted altogether.

The importance of a teacher's questioning techniques and structuring of group activity is exemplified by Ofsted comments (2001q) about effective 16–19 teaching in Sociology. It is reported that 16–19 teachers should exhibit challenge and high expectations through the questioning strategies they use, through their management of discussion and when reinforcing and extending the learning of individual students. Ineffective teaching is characterised as the teacher allowing students' own attitudes to be expressed and described. Far more effective is when the teacher can sharply focus pair work or group discussion, emphasising the practising of key terms and the reflection on reading and research.

While it is acknowledged that teacher exposition can be acceptable, and indeed effective to map out a difficult topic for students, and a brief burst of dictation can explain new terms, extensive dictation can be uninspiring. Used too much it can prevent understanding in depth, and can replicate material that students would be better off consulting for themselves.

In Business Education, Ofsted reports (2001c) that the most effective teaching occurs in discussion if students are motivated and if teachers can intervene to ensure discussion is of the highest quality. Rather than dictating, teachers are recommended to ask students to summarise main points for themselves and share them, with the teacher asking questions to check understanding before moving on. Dictation is considered to inhibit students from thinking for themselves, because it implies a kind of spoon-feeding.

Group work is important if it allows the exploration of higher level challenging questions, because such active learning can stimulate thought and change attitudes amongst students. One problem is that the loss of authority can worry inexperienced teachers. You might be put off by the threat of a noisy 16–19 class when colleagues observing might expect quiet in A level or AVCE lessons. But group work is an important corrective to the over-reliance on didactic delivery of teacher-dominated 16–19 lessons.

GENDER IMBALANCE IN THE 16–19 CLASSROOM

Unlike arrangements in most co-educational compulsory education, in which schools usually seek to balance equally the proportion of male and female pupils in a class, the situation in 16–19 classrooms can be very different. Students have a pretty free choice to study whatever subjects they like, once they have satisfied entry requirements and assuming their institution organises the curriculum flexibly. There is no attempt to balance 16–19 classes on gender lines. The result will be that some 16–19 teachers will be working with a perfectly reasonable and 'normal' balance of male and female students, whereas others will be working with very imbalanced classes, or sometimes single-sex classes.

This gender imbalance amongst pupils choosing specific A level subjects (Watson et al. 1994), with boys opting for sciences and girls for English and associated 'literary' studies, remained constant in A level over the period 1970 to 1995, despite the introduction of a common curriculum in GCSE (Brown 2001). The implication for trainee teachers and NQTs who are otherwise working in co-educational 11–16 classes is significant. There is little evidence that mentors and trainees or NQTs engage in discussion about appropriate pedagogic strategies for single-sex or gender-imbalanced 16–19 classes.

Preparing for this potential imbalance can be vital, as the behaviour of groups of students in such settings, or of individual 'isolated' students, can be a challenge if you are seeking active involvement in classroom activities. For example, male students continue to predominate in Maths, Physics, Chemistry and Information Technology. They are of course subjects in which male teachers predominate too. One resultant danger can be an overly jokey, blokeish banter running as a commentary during lessons, which can exclude female students and at the very least make them feel uncomfortable. It can also cause subsequent problems for other teaching colleagues. Female students may, in such circumstances, appear very passive learners, unwilling (rather than unable) to respond to direct or whole-class questions. Business Education teachers are admonished (Ofsted 2001c) to take steps to avoid neglecting the less assertive female students. It is worth taking a few minutes to consider how we all include passive students in our 16–19 teaching.

Conversely, female students predominate in many Arts and languages classes. This can result, teachers and trainee teachers report, in a culture of quiet note-taking, and of students effectively waiting to be told what to think. At the same time, the minority male students might be seen to bask in exhibiting an immature approach to advanced study. You may find oral contributions from male students in such classes to be highly engaged (but they can also be disruptive and irrelevant). You may also find unhelpful attitudes like an unwillingness to pick up a pen and take notes, despite being asked. These sometimes have to be challenged head on. You need to create a framework to prepare all students to feel secure in a whole-class discussion. This framing should ensure that all understand the conceptual and technical requirements underpinning the topic to be discussed. Without that security, students might respond in a negative way in a discussion, drifting uncertainly in a purposeless exchange.

How can male and female students be drawn into becoming effective learners when gender imbalance affects the learning dynamic of the class? Ofsted (2001a) suggests that questioning skills have to be used skilfully to probe and extend the learning of all students. However, there is a tendency for inexperienced 16–19 teachers to use questioning to merely test recall or to seek 'pseudo-involvement'.

You need to be particularly alert to the relative performance of male and female students in their 16–19 classrooms. Does active engagement in lessons equate with high grades, and are those evenly distributed? Are passive students more likely to drop out, and are those retention rates evenly distributed across male and female students?

Ofsted reports (2001g) that 16–19 English teachers should be alert to lower attaining male students offering less detailed answers than females. They should also be conscious of the style and vocabulary offered by both male and female students in critical writing, and their respective reading skills. Teachers are advised to intervene in male students' superficial or facile assumptions about major dimensions of a text. So gender imbalance can be an issue affecting behaviour and learning in the 16–19 classroom.

BEHAVIOUR IN THE 16–19 CLASSROOM

One positive aspect of teaching 16–19 students is that, having chosen to stay in education and being free from the shackles of the National Curriculum subjects they were forced to do, many students can be enthusiastic, committed and motivated. However, not all will have acquired the skills of being independent, autonomous learners. Not all will be motivated, and not all will be academic high fliers.

As a 16–19 teacher you will need to exhibit confidence in your approach to all students, and to understand as quickly as possible the dynamics of the group. You need to think carefully about your own use of language. How can you organise the social dynamic of the 16–19 classroom to prevent behavioural crises occurring? How can you speak supportively to students who may need some confidence rebuilding from a previous negative experience of learning? How can you encourage the good behaviour expected, while correcting anything unacceptable? How can consequences of any poor behaviour be administered?

Prevention is the best way to counter unacceptable behaviour. In 16–19 teaching, this can take the form of:

- careful lesson planning which takes account of differentiation
- organising room furniture in a suitable way for intended activities (especially group work)
- checking that technology or practical equipment works beforehand
- making a purposeful start to the lesson
- agreeing clear and positive rules with your students (it is vital they take responsibility for behaviour boundaries themselves)
- making the consequences of any infringements explicit
- developing clear routines
- finishing each lesson in a well-ordered way.

Behaviour management is crucial in 16–19 education. Without it, problems in the classroom will lead to ineffective learning, regardless of whether the resources you provide are interesting or whether the objectives of the lesson are sound.

Inexperienced teachers can often possess unrealistic expectations about the likely behaviour of 16–19 students. This is important because inflated expectations about compliant behaviour and positive attitudes to learning can falsely inform planning for 16–19 classes. Challenges to this misjudged expectation can throw the most carefully prepared lesson and can spoil the effectiveness of an intended learning experience. The need to manage 'on-task' behaviour, particularly but not exclusively in Year 12, is paramount if efficient use of the limited teaching time available is to be sustained.

To do this effectively as a 16–19 teacher, you need to use rapport, empathy and humour rather than confrontation and overt disciplinary measures. If an individual student is dominating a group or class in an unacceptable manner, it is far better to avoid a public slanging match. It is much better to:

- communicate any personal rules about student behaviour (and share these with colleagues)
- criticise the behaviour rather than the person
- be consistent and fair to all students
- avoid sarcasm or making the perpetrator look foolish.

Behaviour problems can often be prevented if a teacher prepares to use a range of different strategies with which to engage all the students in a class. Once the initial ice-breaking activities are out of the way, it is useful to have the following interactions in the repertoire:

- Active listening
- Clarifying
- Reflecting back
- Summarising
- Advising
- Target setting
- Empathising
- Probing

It is also worth considering if students expect to contribute to their own learning. You can deliberately make use of students' previously acquired knowledge, and you should report back to the class in an explanatory rather than a factual manner. You should always be prepared to challenge poor punctuality and a failure to hand in work on time as unacceptable behaviours.

If the behaviour of a given student or group of students becomes problematic, and is affecting the learning of the rest of the class as well as your relationship with the group, it is imperative to act. But there is a fine balance to be struck with 16–19 students. It is important to let students avoid the embarrassment of losing face. First-name terms make this easier to achieve, but physical contact should be avoided with students or their property. Minor misdemeanours can often be deflected with eye contact, non-verbal communication, a change of position, or humour (but never sarcasm). If you spot an individual doing the right thing in behaviour terms, reward them with a positive word.

More serious problems require a reprimand in which the seriousness matches the transgression. Such procedures should be introduced as early as possible, and integrated explicitly into classroom routines. Consistently challenging behaviour should be dealt with formally in line with institutional guidelines (check you know what these are and which senior member of staff is responsible for administering them).

In 16–19 education serious discipline problems should be rare, but they are not unknown. It is important to emphasise the positive things you can do to limit the chance of poor behaviour occurring. Make sure that students are always engaged in purposeful activity and that time is being used in a focused way. It helps to reiterate timings for particular activities. Make your feedback inclusive, and challenge your students intellectually. And use questioning constructively to manage the class.

ICT AND THE 16–19 TEACHER

Active learning can also depend on the resources at the teacher's disposal, and how they are used. ICT in 16–19 teaching is a good example of this. Ask yourself the key question: what is the purpose of your use of ICT (ILT in colleges)? Is your purpose to enhance and extend your teaching? This might be important with pressure to reduce 16–19 contact time in many institutions. If so, your approach will incorporate ICT as a stimulus, rather than bolting it on as an afterthought. Of course 16–19 teachers are now able to access a greater range of electronic teaching materials, some (though certainly not all) of a high quality. But as well as the material resources, ICT affects the approach you take to teaching. You can perhaps start to think about adapting teaching to meet individual student needs, and to take more account of different learning styles. It can also mean there is more time for teacher talk, or teacher interaction with individuals and small groups. You can perhaps share resources and planning approaches more freely with colleagues. And critically, to aid retention, you can keep in contact with students, supporting them when they are not in lessons, or not even in the institution, and providing feedback online. This of course raises complex contractual issues in relation to student contact, but it would be a shame if teachers new to 16–19 teaching did not lead the way in the intelligent use of ICT to support student learning.

However, you must be alert to merely showing off how up-to-date you are, with fantastic new gizmos or software you have acquired. Such flashy use of ICT will in the end be merely decorative and will contribute little to the learning of all students. Teachers also need to consider how to support those drawbacks students encounter when using ICT. There are too many tales of students failing to submit A level projects through hard disk crashes, loss of files or printer problems. There are also too many examples of students investing hours and hours in using ICT for presentation when marks are then lost for inadequate analysis or thin content.

Ask yourself another question: how does your use of ICT contribute to students taking responsibility for their own learning? Does it maximise student learning, by complementing their understanding? Does it aid in the retention of students, particularly in that sticky first term of Year 12 when they can wobble, confronted as they are with the demands of longer and more analytical advanced level work. In answer to that, it is important to make explicit the idea of access to a greater range of current resources, and the opportunity to engage in synchronous (real-time) and asynchronous e-conference discussions with students in other institutions (both across the UK and the rest of the world). The considerable fillip given to the quality of presentation of students' work is as important as the enhanced coverage of specifications possible. It is also a pragmatic fact that larger teaching groups in Year 12 can make teachers' marking loads prohibitively onerous. Can use of ICT build a little more flexibility into the assessment load?

Integrating ICT into 16–19 teaching can have a positive impact on student motivation. If tasks are differentiated, individual students can work in a more autonomous way, managing their own pace of learning and taking pride in the appearance of their work. It does mean careful preparation has to take place so that students understand the kind of approach they need to take when answering questions in an electronic environment. There is also often a bonus of collaborative approaches to problem solving, especially when more expert students can iron out technical problems for their peers.

If your focus is on ICT in 16–19 teaching, the first thing to consider is how you can mediate the mass of electronic information available to students. Is your use of ICT synchronous? If so, this will include strategies that may add to the repertoire of teaching strategies, such as the use of interactive whiteboards and powerpoint presentation in the classroom. These will affect your role as teacher, shifting the relationship with students to one of facilitator, supporting group working and providing surgeries for individual students. Your use of ICT could equally be asynchronous, in the students' own time, providing feedback online via email contact to support learning and monitor progress. This can eventually save time in monitoring progress.

Examples of effective ICT in 16–19 teaching:

- Library resource centre: teachers should go out of their way to draw on the resources and skills of e-library and e-learning centres in their institutions. These usually house a significant number of computer work stations providing online access. These should not be on the margins of teaching and learning, but central to planning and delivery. Library or learning centre staff are invariably only too pleased to offer skills workshops (such as how to do bibliographic searches for projects) for 16–19 teachers and their students. This is a good way to integrate these skills into teaching (in a way that bolt-on Key Skills too often do not) and to meet some of the AS/A specifications.

- How effective are you at teaching and supporting your students to use the internet effectively for structured searching of relevant sites and resources? Do you provide carefully selected and vetted lists of suitable sites to which students are first directed? Do you have a chance to check and update them, given the transient nature of much of the material on the web? The important thing is to get your students to use the web intelligently, using search engines and key word searches efficiently. Important sites identified by you can be incorporated into all the teaching materials you develop. Do you provide links to newsgroups in subject specialisms? How good is your own use of the internet to support your teaching? Can you model that to your students? This is increasingly important given the AS/A2 specifications which emphasise research skills in using the internet.

- Email: do you utilise fully the potential of regular, structured email contact with your 16–19 students, without drowning in a barrage of what can appear constant email pressure? Do you receive and return assignments electronically? Do you use email to keep in contact with students who are on study leave revising, or who are ill and missing lessons? This is an excellent and efficient way to share resources amongst students in your group, and to ensure that every student has received relevant notes. For example, group work can easily be shared with the teacher emailing copies of the various powerpoint presentations to the whole class. Mail groups can be set up to remind students about impending deadlines. Students can prepare for taught sessions by enquiring what to read beforehand, or follow up what they have not understood, or seek clarification of homework tasks.

- Powerpoint: to what extent are you making use of powerpoint in your teaching? Needing just a laptop and a ceiling-housed projector, this has the advantage of greater clarity than most OHTs or notes on a traditional whiteboard (which too often appear illegible, or remain left on too long). Powerpoint can be used very effectively in combination with other classroom aids including material on CD-Rom. For example, the interactive white-board, found in an increasing number of teaching rooms, can be used to capture impromptu oral contributions and summarise discussion points, as well as offering pre-written bullets. Teaching part of a lesson to a powerpoint presentation enables a 16–19 teacher to impart key elements of a course, without overloading students. Brevity can aid focus, directness can aid clarity. The best examples utilise a large font size with big borders and lots of spacing. Adding point by point on a powerpoint slide is far more effective than preparing an OHT which has to be covered and revealed point by point. The ubiquitous handout can be greatly improved by the kind of gapped skeleton completed by the teacher summarising student input. A printout of the presentation can form an accessible and clear revision tool. And of course a teacher can retain and easily amend powerpoint presentations by keeping them on disk.

- Students can be organised to work in small groups to prepare a powerpoint presentation, drawing together ideas and summarising key points as concisely as possible. They can then be put into 'teaching mode', to deliver their findings to the rest of the class, and can indeed be assessed by their peers for the quality of learning experienced.

- School/college-wide intranet: can be a really effective use of ICT to support learning when 16–19 teachers provide case-study resources (perhaps organised through an interactive multimedia database), web links or assignment titles on the internal network accessible to all students. All lessons can in theory be stored if word processed, allowing students opportunities to go over replicated tasks again and again, whether from a learning resource centre, or using remote access (home?) to facilitate deeper learning. Student-generated presentations can also be easily disseminated in this way. An intranet can also house pre-course study materials which students can be encouraged (or required) to engage with as a bridge from GCSE work in Year 11. If linked to a dedicated, subject or course-specific conference, students can post responses in online discussion threads. Teachers can also put 'practice' tests online, so that students nearing terminal AS examinations in Year 12, for example, can engage in revision in their own time and not take up important class time. Teachers can mark online. An intranet can also be useful if a member of staff has to be absent. There can be filtered links to specified websites.

- CAD/CAM: an important component in many design-based courses, but is there a coherent justification for over-elaborate and complex usage by teachers or students in every 16–19 Design class? If you are using a piece of software in your teaching to perform tedious statistical calculations, or construct graphs which alter as data changes, be explicit that you are using it to complement your teaching. Spreadsheets, used to produce graphs and charts, can be a huge asset to the efficient use of teacher time and to student presentation skills. In addition, the use of databases by students can enable large amounts of information to be shared across a class, with scope for different forms of analysis and manipulation.

- Digitising images: increasingly part of professional practice in Art and Design. Specialist teachers should integrate digital art skills by encouraging students to store and generate images, and to undertake research and investigation. Linked to desk-top-publishing applications, increasingly high quality and individualised documents can be produced, integrating photos and data into text in all 16–19 subjects and courses.

Conclusion: ICT and active learning

As secondary schools and colleges increasingly share videoconferencing facilities, and as the use of laptops by students and their teachers becomes easier due to wireless technology, active learning will take on a very different meaning. All 16–19 students may be working directly on to their laptops in the not too distant future, taking and sharing notes and collaborating on presentations. Active learning will become much more significantly about engagement in learning tasks in a wired community. The 16–19 teacher will, in the future, support individuals and groups of students in a more balanced mix of 'traditional' directed teaching, group activities and electronic involvement.

But we are not there yet, and we have seen much money spent on computer suites in schools and colleges that do not do the job envisaged for them, becoming all too quickly redundant. We do not yet have all 16–19 students possessing highly developed ICT skills, so there certainly remains a need for keyboard skills (at the very least) to be supported in all institutions, whether by distance learning or face-to-face tuition. We have yet to solve how to verify coursework produced on ICT that has not been plagiarised. It is also worth remembering the assumptions we might make about ICT in terms of students' own word-processing skills. While some 16–19 students may already be making notes in lessons on to laptops, utilising sophisticated electronic approaches to drafting essays or building their own glossaries or date lines in databases, others may have no access to ICT at home, or may lack keyboard skills or broader computer literacy. How can we find out, and how can we then support the development of all students' ICT skills?

It would also be erroneous to make overly generous assumptions about access to good ICT facilities in any particular 16–19 teaching room, or indeed across whole departments in some schools or colleges. If in doubt, school or college libraries often provide a vital, up-to-date ICT resource for 16–19 teaching, and it is always worth cultivating the colleagues responsible for such information centres to explain your teaching needs.

The lesson seems to be that, despite enthusiasts and proselytisers for ICT in 16–19 teaching, and despite the fascinating technologies targeted at classroom teaching, small ICT developments, introduced relatively slowly and with adequate time to evaluate, are most likely to lead to more effective teaching. Even then, too many institutions have stinted on staff training in the use of the new technologies, and so impact is often uneven. Whole-school or whole-college support is vital for accredited programmes like CLAIT or ECDL.

There can be little doubt that we are on the cusp of a revolution in 16–19 teaching. ICT already can improve student tracking, and can improve work submission and presentation. Younger teachers will see the approaches that are effective shift over the next generation as ICT becomes more embedded. Be open to the challenge. But remember that active learning still relies on a human dimension, whether the 16–19 teacher is planning face-to-face or virtual interactions to engage students.

HEADLINES

- 16–19 students learn effectively from group work if it is well planned.
- Gender issues are significant factors in effective 16–19 learning.
- On-task behaviour cannot be assumed in all 16–19 classrooms.
- Effective 16–19 teachers embrace the potential of ICT, but only where it enhances what they do in the classroom.

8 The importance of the tutor role in 16–19 teaching

Qualifying to Teach Standards

1.4   *Communicate sensitively and effectively with parents and carers, recognising their roles in pupils' learning.*

2.6   *Understand their responsibilities under the SEN code of practice and how to seek advice from specialists on less common types of special educational needs.*

3.1.5   *Able to plan for opportunities for pupils to learn in out-of-school contexts, such as school visits, museums, theatres, field work and . . . employment-based settings with the help of other staff where appropriate.*

FENTO Standards

E   *Providing learners with support*

      E1   *induct learners into the organisation*

      E2   *provide effective learning support*

      E3   *ensure access to guidance opportunities for learners*

      E4   *provide personal support for learners*

OBJECTIVES

Reading this chapter and engaging actively with the tasks will enable you to:

- understand the importance of the 16–19 tutor role
- consider the balance in the role between support for HE and career entry
- reflect on the key aspects of a support role for 16–19 learners
- implement teaching strategies which will produce evidence to meet QTS Standards 1.4, 2.6, 3.1.5, and FENTO Standards E1–4.

IS THE 16–19 TUTOR'S ROLE FULLY ESTABLISHED?

At 16–19, tutoring is vitally important. To perform the role effectively can be immensely satisfying for an individual teacher. Responsibilities can range from writing UCAS references, to ongoing academic monitoring, to providing a PHSE or General Studies programme. A tutor can make a significant contribution to the educational experience of 16–19 learners, can aid retention and can improve outcomes in terms of course grades, examination results and progression.

Ofsted (2001r) is extremely interested in 16–19 retention. It certainly reports as a concern any centre in which 16–19 retention falls below 80 per cent. This issue has a significant impact on the work of tutors. It is an indication that the course or programme choice made by students is an important focus for tutor support. This is especially true for ongoing subject choice during the early weeks of Year 12 when the culture shock of new approaches and new opportunities (to say nothing of greater academic demands) is at its highest.

Unfortunately, for trainee secondary or FE teachers, or for inexperienced teachers given a 16–19 tutor group, the role of the tutor in 16–19 education is often unclear. In contrast, tutoring in 11–16 education has a far more unambiguous definition (although that is not without its problems). Pastoral responsibility for a group of 11–16 learners is prescribed in reasonably explicit terms in most schools. This would include responsibility for monitoring regular and punctual attendance, links with parents or guardians, oversight of discipline issues and academic progress against explicit targets. In addition, programmes of PHSE and careers education are usually organised on a cross-school programme and delivered or facilitated by 11–16 tutors. From the learners' point of view, the key is that in most schools the 11–16 tutor will follow the same group through their compulsory secondary education as (often) the sole point of teacher continuity. Hence, the role has the potential to be a vital one in supporting and enhancing pupils' experience of learning in the final phase of compulsory schooling.

In general, 16–19 tutoring is less clearly conceptualised, despite exemplary work from some individuals in some centres. Too often, the contact with 16–19 students is in brief registration periods when little support for individual learners can be offered. This is low-status time in 16–19 education, and can often be treated grudgingly, as a necessary chore by students and tutors. Where tutorial programmes are in place, they can appear an irrelevant bolt-on for students, and some tutors might approach tutoring in a half-hearted way because they have little ownership of what they are required to do. At its worse, this can result in a lack of planning, last-minute resource preparation and inadequately structured individual follow-up, all of which would be unacceptable in the substantive teaching role.

Tutoring at 16–19 can appear a management afterthought, and can therefore become a low priority for busy teachers. Indeed, in some schools a 16–19 tutor might have no

16–19 teaching at all, and might not otherwise be based in a sixth-form area. In some colleges, a tutor might have no 'teaching' contact with their tutees. This makes building any sort of relationship with a group of students, or individuals within that group, very difficult.

The skills of the effective 16–19 tutor are a refinement of some aspects of good teaching. They can be characterised by: an open and exploratory approach to discussions with groups or individuals in which a non-judgemental stance is taken. Equal opportunities should be modelled rather than 'taught'. When tutors question, they should focus on learning experiences, course progress and future goals. They should not involve more private aspects of students' lives unless raised by students. Even then, discretion and ethical considerations have to be taken into account. Students should understand that as a tutor you are not in the role of a trained counsellor. There should not be 'closed-door' confidential exchanges without the presence of a colleague. Advice about the use of school, college or external support services should be given, rather than attempts to deal with situations beyond a tutor's responsibility.

Given the broader range of learners choosing to remain in 16–19 education, and given the increasing emphasis on learner support in tertiary education, there is undoubtedly an important guidance and advice role that a 16–19 tutor needs to be confident about providing. Part of this is looking outwards to the progression opportunities available for students.

PREPARATION FOR HIGHER EDUCATION: THE 16–19 TUTOR'S ROLE

Tutors can play an important role in the expectations 16–19 students have of Higher Education. On the one hand, a Year 12 student with potential who is not considering applying (perhaps horizons are limited if no one in their family has ever applied, perhaps financial considerations are impinging, perhaps they lack confidence in their abilities at a higher level, perhaps university is seen as something for posh white people) might be linked to a Year 13 'study buddy' following similar subjects who *is* applying (Marland 2003). Alternatively, a mentor student from a local university or former pupil currently in HE might become involved. Either option may need instigating by a proactive tutor.

Tutors in 16–19 education also have a unique role in preparing students for, and advising students on, higher education entry. This can involve the provision of practical materials with associated activities, visits to HE fairs and open days, and (increasingly important) advice for students (and parents) worried about incurring debt and the cost of HE. Tutors may wish to invite a former student in to speak about their experience of financial pressures on HE study. In addition, support for the preparation of Records of Achievement and curriculum vitae, not to mention the ubiquitous UCAS form, can become a significant element of a 16–19 tutor's role. The last needs generic tutor input as well as comments on the elegance and efficiency of written drafts.

Tutors may well find themselves dealing with stressed students as pressures mount at the start of Year 13 on predicted grades for HE entry. Unfortunately, there is too much evidence of some institutions and some subject teachers (to say nothing of some parents) contributing to a kind of hysteria around HE entry. Tutors need to develop expertise in advising students about progression opportunities to HE, but the kind of support offered needs to be realistic and often quite pragmatic (checking drafts of personal statements, channelling information about open days to interested individuals, clarifying advantages and disadvantages of combined degrees over single-subject degrees or articulating the most effective use of a gap year as a bridge to HE).

For students who are considering an application to university, awareness has to be raised at the time of course choice that there is a huge gap between the curriculum in school and university. For example, even students successful in English A level can be surprised and shocked by the number of texts to be read in the first year of undergraduate study, by the level of response required in higher education, by the introduction of hitherto unencountered literary theory. And all of this with reduced contact time to support learning. Such transitions need to be prepared for, and the 16–19 tutor can be in a strong position to provide this. For example, tutors might organise visiting HE speakers to provide a sample of university life to stimulate curiosity.

Tutors need to prepare students for any Higher Education interviews, utilising role play and inviting all students to prepare exemplar questions. Some thought might be given to video- or audio-taping practice interviews for the benefit of other students. It is also worth considering if the kind of study skills vital for HE (taking notes in lectures, speed reading text books) should be supported by 16–19 tutors through Key Skills to complement subject-related skills.

Ofsted is also very interested in the clarity of advice offered to students about 'cashing-in' AS level grades. This has been a contentious area for advice since the introduction of AS in Curriculum 2000 which tightened and realigned resit opportunities to allow only one. Each institution will provide its own guidance, so make sure you are clear what this is.

THE TUTOR ROLE IN SUPPORTING 16–19 CAREERS EDUCATION

The experience of learners in 11–16 education is that most secondary schools at least attempt to plan a reasonably coherent programme of careers education for KS3 and KS4. The coverage is far less clear in 16–19 education, with support often dependent upon a student taking the initiative and requesting support from an external agency. GNVQ and AVCE students may be more fortunate, since their teachers may integrate careers education through their curriculum delivery, and vocationally relevant work-experience should offer more learning opportunities than work-experience in Years

10 or 11. If you are providing work-experience for your students, do check that the appropriate support mechanisms are in place.

In general, tutors need to become expert in their understanding of the sources of advice available to 16–19 students, and to be well-informed about school or college systems. This may impact on the tutor's role early in Year 12, as subject choices and subject changes are scheduled. For example, links with the Connexions service (Ofsted 2001d) need to be made and sustained to provide access to informed careers advice to ensure that students are on the right course or programme to meet their career aspirations. The Connexions service is an integrated provision of forty-seven partnerships (sharing the same geographical boundaries as the Learning Skills Councils). Formerly, separate provision was made by the Careers Service, Social and Youth Services, and Health and Drug Education, but Connexions is an attempt at 'joined-up thinking' to offer more effective and efficient support. Personal advisers working in schools and colleges differentiate by supporting specific age groups (for example, 16–19) or individual students with multiple problems. Tutors should be confident about initiating support for their pastoral responsibilities, and seeking impartial advice for their students.

It is also worth a reminder that not all Year 13 students will wish to go to university (at least not in the short term). Tutors may also wish to invite in a previous student who did not choose to go on to Higher Education. They can be briefed to address a tutor group about the financial issues and advantages of working at 18 or 19.

I can recall, for example, while plenty of my friends and peers in the sixth form were applying to university, I was not. I half wanted to but I was more aware of my parents' concern about the cost of studying. For them, it was difficult to equate the theoretical economic benefit of study with the loss of three years of potential earnings. I could not articulate an argument to convince myself, so I did not attempt to persuade them. I certainly do not regret this, but I do wonder if my Year 13 teachers saw me differently. Did I need good grades if I was going out to work after A levels? I might be unfair, but when the A level grades came out (posted to my home in self-addressed envelopes, arriving on different days!) I was already outside the education system. There was no support for what, looking back, were certainly lower-than-expected grades in two of my three subjects. This should not be true today, and 16–19 tutors should be prepared for a pro-active role each summer.

Tutors might also need their radar attuned as hormones and a late-night clubbing social life kick in for their tutees. This can lead to some students struggling to cope with studying if they are drinking alcohol and/or taking recreational drugs. Sexual concerns can also impact on the lives of 16–19 students and negatively affect their learning. Sensitive support to individuals, and carefully planned discussion with tutor groups, together with informed contact with specialist local agencies, is as far as most 16–19 tutors would be advised to go.

STUDENTS WORKING PART-TIME: THE 16–19 TUTOR'S ROLE

The guidance role can also manifest itself in more individualised monitoring of student progress. This can surface in a number of unpredictable ways, for example, when Year 12 students struggle to get to classes or complete homework, exhausted from the pressure of part-time employment. Tutors can be in the front line, dealing with issues for students attempting to combine full-time study with part-time work. It is worth remembering that there are a number of positives to do with young adults taking on paid work for a few hours per week:

- Working part-time can teach students to organise themselves.
- Working part-time can help students become more self-reliant.
- Students can gain both useful work experience and a link to the adult world outside school or college.
- For some individuals, it is only the opportunity to earn some money which enables them to stay on in education.

Of course these need to be balanced with a number of well-publicised fears:

- Part-time work leaves insufficient time for adequate study.
- Students can become too tired and find themselves unable to concentrate properly in class if they are working part-time.
- Classes may be skipped in order to work as the employer demands, or students may arrive late for classes.

Recent research (Payne 2003) presents fifteen hours' part-time work per week as the critical point. Paid work for a few hours per week has a negligible effect on A level grades. If 16–19 students are working in excess of fifteen hours per week, it can significantly reduce grades. For example, there is evidence that a Year 12 student working sixteen to twenty hours per week could be expected to drop one grade in AS level.

More female than male students are likely to work part-time (but they work fewer hours). The average number of hours worked by 16–19 students is twelve hours, but the better the GCSE results, the fewer hours a 16–19 student is likely to work. It also seems that if a student is not working while in Year 12, they are more likely to stay into Year 13. (Although for some students in Year 12, working part-time could indicate a relatively low commitment to full-time education.)

The real issue for tutors to watch is those 16–19 students working long hours (more than fifteen per week) during term time. You might share with such students that a drop of one grade at A level, on what might be expected, is the likely result. Also, the negative impact takes effect during Year 13 at a lower number of hours compared to Year 12. It is worth exploring if your school or college offers clear guidance to students and their parents about part-time working. Are links made at a senior level with local retail outlets, (which tend to be the main sources of employment for 16–19 students) to establish sensible working expectations for full-time students?

The research has been unable to establish a correlation between part-time hours worked and performance on AVCE courses.

16–19 SEN STUDENTS: THE TUTOR'S ROLE

Tutors have a particularly important role in supporting the transition of students with a Special Educational Need into post-compulsory education. This can involve links with school or college support services for those students with a statement of SEN, and with the Connexions service for those students without a statement. It is worth all 16–19 teachers noting that in a recent study (Polat *et al.* 2001) 56 per cent of a large sample of pupils with SEN followed the full National Curriculum in Year 11, yet only 16 per cent of SEN pupils stayed in education after 16. Despite this, the widening access agenda in higher education has led to an increase in the number of students with disabilities and learning difficulties being admitted to university.

Of those students entering 16–19 education with a Special Educational Need, twice as many are likely to be boys rather than girls. The male students are likely to perform less well than their female counterparts. Tutors might need to at least be aware of the range of possible disabilities, and to liaise with a SENCO or learning-support assistant for further insight into likely need. The tutor can then act as a conduit for effective teaching strategies for relevant subject teachers. For example, does a 16–19 student in your tutor group have:

- A moderate or mild learning difficulty?
- Emotional and behavioural difficulties (as in a condition like Attention Deficit Hyperactive Disorder, ADHD)?
- Dyslexia or dyspraxia?
- A sensory, physical or medical difficulty?
- Speech/language difficulties?
- Autism/Aspergers syndrome?
- School phobia?

Case study: how might 16–19 tutors support students with SEN?

Attention Deficit Disorder (ADD) is a condition that involves a shortening of the ability to maintain span of attention and difficulty in concentrating. Those with ADD often have difficulties with information involving sequencing (retaining information in the right order, for example spelling patterns) and process information slowly. Someone with ADD effectively diverts some of their ability into utilisation of coping strategies (which can be fatiguing), so they learn in school or college with what is 'left' after coping with the perceived complexities of life. The typical ADD individual is usually socially immature and is often quiet in school, in contrast to pupils with ADHD. Performance in class and external tests is likely to be inconsistent (reflecting a significant gap between verbal and non-verbal IQ), but can restore after the age of 16.

For example, Xavier is now 16. He was (finally) diagnosed with ADD five months before he was due to sit GCSE examinations at his comprehensive school. He is currently in the sixth form, studying three AS levels in History, Government and Politics, and Communication Studies, as well as resitting GCSE Maths.

At primary school his parents worried about his poor progress, but were regularly told unsympathetically 'he's a boy' as a justification for his lack of development. Commenting that he knew the capital city and flag of every country but still couldn't read, his parents were told 'It's a pity he doesn't know something useful'.

At middle school he was assessed and placed on Stage 3 of the Individual Education Plan (IEP). Progress began to be made thanks to the help he received from individual teachers who recognised that with a little extra consideration he could achieve something approaching his potential. Examples of this included making doubly certain (by checking) that he had understood what was required on every task. By the time he left middle school, he came out at a Stage 1 IEP, and on the teacher's recommendation his parents agreed to him being removed from the special needs register entirely as he had begun to make such progress and would not want to be labelled SEN in his big new comprehensive.

Initially, he coped reasonably well at secondary school. But from Year 9 to the start of Year 11 he made little progress across all subjects. His written work continued to be scrappy, he was poorly organised, he lost materials and items of clothing and never seemed to grasp homework tasks. His parents continued to attend every parents' evening, each time commenting on his lack of homework, his inability to communicate what tasks he had been asked to do, his failure to make progress. Teachers continued to praise his oral ability (he can sound very engaged, well-informed and able), but lamented his written output and lack of homework. He was easily distracted, and seemed unable to understand or to action what was required of him in class. His written work (presentation, spelling and quantity) had never reflected his oral ability and he was told he was lazy if he did not submit written work that was considered to be at an appropriate standard. Despite parental requests, no teacher contacted his home to clarify homework due. By the start of Year 11, it was apparent that Xavier was a borderline D candidate in every one of his eleven GCSEs.

Towards the end of the Christmas term of Year 11, a critical incident occurred. Xavier was so frustrated at being singled out and told off for not working in a Science lesson (when he was trying really hard and other pupils were talking and messing about) that something inside him snapped. He ran out of the class, barging the male teacher out of the way in the process, and rushed all the way home. He spent the next twenty-four hours weeping at home and repeatedly punching the wall of his room (by this age he was a big lad). His acute frustration at the gap between what he perceived as his intellectual abilities, what he perceived as working hard and the injustice of disappointing test scores and predicted grades burst out. He could no longer deal with the injustice of schooling.

His parents felt they had to intervene. Finding an educational psychologist on the internet, they arranged and paid for a private consultation to provide an educational assessment to offer a diagnosis of his learning needs, and a set of recommendations to make to his school. They also paid for a session in which the psychologist briefed Xavier on the significance of the findings for his future learning career.

Recommendations included:

1   Reduce workload (he was disapplied from GCSE Spanish and given some one-on-one support in the time freed up to help organise remaining coursework).
2   General encouragement (some teachers, on reading the report, took a far more sympathetic stance towards supporting his learning. It seemed to help that it now had a medical name.)
3   Study Skills (20 per cent extra time provided in GCSE exams, which were sat separately in a quiet room he knew rather than an examination hall to eliminate distractions which might interfere with his concentration).

These interventions were organised by his Year 11 tutor and resulted in a happier pupil and the achievement of two grade B, three grade C and five grade D passes at GCSE. This was enough to enable him to join the sixth form. Here is the summary that his parents provided to the 16–19 tutor on his entry to sixth form:

Xavier was assessed by a Chartered Psychologist following concerns by Year 11 teachers and parents that his oral ability was not matched by his assessed grades in coursework and examinations. ADD was diagnosed when verbal IQ scores significantly outweighed comprehension and performance scores. Essentially, the majority of his mental capacity is taken up with 'coping' with life, so schoolwork uses what capacity is left over. This can lead to fatigue, because his brain has to work harder than others to reach the same level.

Positive learning behaviour to draw on
   i   He can be an engaging conversationalist, an enthusiastic generator of ideas, speaking at length in a dynamic and multi-faceted way.
   ii   He will use his long-term memory to recall former events.
   iii He sees the bigger picture quickly, and can engage in diverse thoughts simultaneously.

How does Xavier's ADD manifest itself?

i   Slow processing of information

ii   Difficulties with sequencing information

iii   Difficulties retaining information in the right order (poor short-term memory)

iv   Inconsistent spelling and test performance (test performances likely to be lower than his true ability)

v   Immature, slow handwriting

vi   Poor planning and organisation

vii   Easily bored

What can teachers do to support Xavier's learning?

i   Teaching style needs to meet his needs (variety, brevity, one-on-one or small-group instruction, tasks and directions broken down into steps)

ii   Teachers need to make organisational interventions (i.e. check that he has written homework down fully and understands what is required)

iii   Encourage him (a positive 'how can I help you remember your homework?' rather than a negative 'when will you remember your homework?')

iv   Persist in teaching him organisational and study skills

v   Can he speak notes into a tape recorder?

vi   Assessment flexibility will need to continue as structured provision in continuous assessment, timed and untimed tests, etc.

In this case, the 16–19 tutor needed to liaise with all relevant subject teachers to ensure they were clear about the kind of classroom strategies that would need to be in place to support Xavier's learning. How confident would you be in the effectiveness of your support in such a situation?

CONCLUSION

The role of the 16–19 tutor is a highly responsible and important one, and not to be taken lightly. To perform the role effectively is immensely satisfying, but equally demanding. It includes:

- pastoral role (induction, welfare links, contact with support staff as necessary)
- student progress monitoring role (liaison between parents/carers and subject teachers, exam entries)
- career links (connecting with relevant Connexions staff)
- Higher Education guidance and advice (up-to-date information, student-centred)
- programme facilitator (PHSE/General Studies or Key Skills).

9   Learning with colleagues: developing a career in 16–19 teaching

Qualifying to Teach Standards

1.7   *Able to improve own teaching by evaluating it, learning from the effective practice of others and from evidence . . . able to take increasing responsibility for their own professional development.*

3.1.4   *Take part in, and contribute to, teaching teams . . . plan for the deployment of additional adults who support pupils' learning.*

3.3.13 *They can work collaboratively with specialist teachers and other colleagues and, with the help of an experienced teacher as appropriate, manage the work of teaching assistants or other adults to enhance pupils' learning.*

FENTO Standards

G   *Reflecting upon and evaluating one's own performance and planning future practice*
    G1   *evaluate one's practice*
    G2   *plan for future practice*
    G3   *engage in continuing professional development*

OBJECTIVES

Reading this chapter and engaging actively with the tasks will enable you to:

- appreciate the need for continuing professional development in 16–19 teaching
- consider how to work effectively in 16–19 teaching teams
- reflect upon career possibilities in 16–19 teaching
- engage with the professional dimension of teaching which will produce evidence to meet QTS Standards 1.7, 3.1.4, 3.3.13, and FENTO Standards G1–3, H1–2.

H   *Meeting professional requirements (a competence underpinning all other processes)*
    H1   *work with a professional value base*
    H2   *conform to agreed codes of practice*

THE IMPORTANCE OF COLLABORATION AMONGST 16–19 TEACHERS

> Changes have been so rapid and demanding [in 16–19 education] . . . that intense continuing professional development, training and learning has been required.
> (Le Versha and Nicholls 2003, p. v)

The overarching intention of this book is that the secret garden of 16–19 teaching can be opened up, and that teachers can be encouraged to support one another in developing their own repertoire of effective teaching strategies in this phase. Although the significant national reforms on 16–19 education have been imposed from above, the most effective teachers have the confidence to interpret the policies and to mould them to best suit the local circumstances and contexts of their students. Fullan (2001) argues that only at the individual and team level can multiple innovations (like those that have affected 16–19 education since 2000) be managed. The social complexities of an innovation like Curriculum 2000 mean that larger scale attempts to handle the changes are likely to fail. It is the frequent interactions with 16–19 colleagues in a collaborative culture that are most likely to bring about effective teaching.

There is a significant reason for devoting a chapter to 16–19 teachers working with colleagues. New curriculum and assessment regimes require teachers to plan and develop courses together as teams. The days of the maverick, unaccountable 16–19 teacher, inspiring or boring generations of students behind closed doors are fast disappearing. It is important that teachers continue to inspire students, but this must be shared with other colleagues. For new 16–19 teachers, it is imperative to evaluate the effectiveness of materials, planning, sequencing and teaching activities. With the new 16–19 arrangements, teachers, departments and institutions need to plan for differing patterns of work, perhaps even across institutions. Hence new 16–19 teachers learn best from one another, and from more experienced colleagues, to improve teaching and learning, to support a culture of extended professionalism, and to support retention.

For teachers new to 16–19 teaching, professional isolation can be a significant problem. In schools, there are few opportunities provided for teachers to collaborate in their 16–19 teaching role. Managers are rarely in a position to provide the practical backing for colleagues to team teach, to observe one another's lessons, to plan sequences of work together, to moderate one another's assessments and to share resources. The situation in colleges is often little better, with resources to support continuing professional development in short supply, and not always targeted towards teaching and learning strategies. It is thus vital for teachers to be proactive about exploiting these opportunities when they do come up, and engineering opportunities themselves where they do not.

The opportunity to see how other colleagues work is crucial, not least to enable you to critique your own taken-for-granted assumptions about effective practice. Often, a colleague's professional interventions can make the familiar unfamiliar. This can impact vicariously on your own approaches. Within your institution, or your own department, the positive benefits of mutual observation of 16–19 teaching, followed by structured discussion, can be immense. Visits to other schools or colleges to observe 16–19 teaching is a rare luxury, yet where such planned activities do take place, they can contribute a vital entitlement to professional development that is focused on teaching and learning.

The most effective professional support for developing a career in 16–19 teaching comes from a shared discourse around professional learning. This invariably depends upon the value system of an institution. Where this culture is strongly established, professional discourse involves open dialogue and discussion about developing and adapting effective practice. It includes purposeful interactions with a teacher's own school or college community, together with external agencies. The kind of conversations that take place are focused on meeting individual and group learning needs, and exploring how to raise standards. In circumstances which are propitious, 16–19 teaching can then become an overt model of good practice, rather than a furtive and enigmatic individual activity behind closed doors.

Often an informal arrangement with a more experienced colleague as a 'post-16 buddy' can get 16–19 professional learning started. The agenda for this might include:

- joint development and planning of new or updated courses
- the improvement of existing resources
- the drafting of new materials
- trialling one another's materials to maximise the chance of the new teacher pitching the resources and related tasks at the appropriate level.

If two teachers are dividing up a 16–19 syllabus between them, the most effective practice emerges when connections are made between theory and evidence across at least two substantive topics. This is best achieved when teachers link their resources and share assessment tasks.

Such collegial learning is based upon co-operative work patterns, and incorporates the importance of the teacher's professional self-esteem. It thrives where there is a common direction, so that ideas and activities are enriched over and above what would occur if a teacher chose, or had no option other than, professional isolation. Where mutually agreed, the relationship can support and challenge teachers, which then models the best teaching. Observation should involve reflection in action, while the following discussion is reflection on action. An experienced 16–19 teacher can help you support strengths and remedy weaknesses in your own 16–19 teaching.

MENTORING AND EFFECTIVE 16–19 TEACHING

Mentoring can and should provide skilled guidance to improve practice, couched in a professional dialogue. This is firmly established in secondary initial teacher education, where mentors are a significant and statutory element in 11–18 school-based training. The mentor role is conceptualised as one provided by an experienced subject specialist, who is expected to provide support and challenge to enable the trainee to meet the Standards. The mentor's role in the assessment of evidence to merit the award of Qualified Teacher status is important, drawing on skilled observation, high quality feedback and regular target setting. Mentors are trained and monitored by the relevant Higher Education Institution or other provider, and Ofsted has the responsibility to quality assure the training that mentors provide. Teaching at 16–19 should be integral to the role, but often is marginalized in training (Butcher 2002, 2003a).

The mentor role is much less firmly established in FE teacher training, where the generic approaches militate against subject-specialist mentors supporting or engaging in a training dialogue. However, criticism by Ofsted (2003) of the lack of subject-based mentoring suggests that the two models of initial training will have to move increasingly closer. This will be especially important as college teachers seek to demonstrate competence. This will involve making conscious choices about what they are to do to achieve key goals, and to determine what is and what is not important in classroom interactions. A mentor, experienced in their own subject, will be a vital sounding board and wise counsel.

Few teachers beyond their induction year are fortunate enough to have a formal mentor arrangement to support their development as an effective 16–19 teacher, so voluntary peer observation to a pre-discussed agenda can be immensely beneficial. Such peer coaching (see Butcher 2000) is established on a more equal footing than mentoring. This can result in exposure to a broader range of teaching strategies which can be tried out, and customised. While collaborating with a subject colleague is the most obvious partnership arrangement, it is not always necessary to link up only to the colleague with whom you share a class. Working with a colleague in the same discipline, or teaching other classes, can produce enhanced awareness of a range of learner needs and different group dynamics, and can be extremely informative.

The even rarer opportunity to follow (shadow) a 16–19 student should not be neglected if this does become available. This can enable an inexperienced 16–19 teacher to observe a broad range of teaching strategies to which their students may be exposed across any week. For example, how often does an A level Maths teacher get a chance to observe some group work in Theatre Studies or Sociology? How often does an A level English teacher get a chance to see some of their students in a Year 13 Chemistry or Physics practical? The benefit is twofold: to gain an insight into effective learning by seeing students learning in different subjects using different strategies, and to evaluate whether those strategies might be worth trying in your own teaching.

16–19 TEAMS

There is no doubt that the department to which you belong can have a huge impact on your professional development opportunities. Unfortunately, teachers seeking enhancement of their 16–19 skills can be at the bottom of the list of priorities when it comes to specific institutional activities. The key for teachers is to seek enhanced opportunities for professional learning, accepting that the impact of these will be varied depending upon individual circumstances. This is where performance review (appraisal) comes in. This entitlement for school teachers to a professional dialogue based on a regular, systematic cycle of target setting and evidence collection is one opportunity to focus on developing 16–19 teaching skills.

For example, 16–19 teachers need to consider whether an expansive, rather than a restricted learning environment can be created in their classroom. This needs a collaborative approach, valuing a wide range of strategies, rather than the narrow range of experiences available if a more individualist approach is taken. All 16–19 teachers will be members of one or more teams, however formally or informally they are constituted. It is worth reflecting how effective those teams are in supporting your own development into becoming an effective 16–19 teacher.

As an illustration of working with colleagues in the 16–19 classroom, Ofsted (2001m) reports an interest in the way 16–19 MFL teachers engage in collaborative work, and how they use access to additional human resources in the classroom. The role of native speakers is considered critical to effective 16–19 language teaching, so teachers should be confident in planning their teaching to incorporate language assistants. It is also recognised that in an increasing number of centres, Year 12 and Year 13 are taught together. This raises the danger of both groups being disadvantaged, but if teachers are able to plan and occasionally teach jointly, a more coherent education programme is likely to result.

Of course all teachers, however experienced, can feel anxious about having another colleague in the classroom observing them. This is often linked to a nervousness associated with being assessed as a trainee, being evaluated as a NQT, and later to the sense of exposure when observation is incorporated as part of appraisal or threshold evidence gathering. For 16–19 teachers this can become bound up with the proprietary feeling of being observed with one's own students in one's own classroom. However, to really develop as a teacher, it is important to overcome those fears and to embrace the potential of mutually agreed professional observation. As long as a focus for the observation is shared and agreed, the benefit can far outweigh the stress.

As a case in point, a trainee teacher should be clear when the observation by a mentor is part of a course evaluation, which will contribute to assessment against the Standards. If so, are there pre-determined targets which should be met? If observed by a line manager as a Newly Qualified Teacher, are you aware how the evidence is to be fed back to you, and how will it influence your induction report? This is crucial, given that NQTs must demonstrate they have continued to meet the Standards for the award of QTS on a consistent basis in an employment context, and met all the induction Standards to satisfactorily complete the induction period (DfEE 1999). This is as true for 16–19 teaching as it is for teaching in the compulsory phase.

If observed by a Head of Department as part of an appraisal or an annual review, how will comments be communicated, and what status will they have? If observed by a peer, how will the colleague provide advice or guidance to assist you evaluate your own teaching? The key is to be comfortable with the professional nature of the dialogue, and to agree a focus that will illuminate an important aspect of 16–19 teaching.

Teachers will need to get used to Ofsted's Common Inspection framework (2001r) for school sixth forms and full-time 16–19 teaching in FE, which will feed into the target setting structured through the local Learning Skills Council. Such observations by inspectors will have more 'bite' than some of the more developmentally focused self-assessment that college teachers have been used to. They will also involve more scrutiny of school-based 16–19 teaching than has previously been the case.

A worthwhile task if evaluating your approach to 16–19 teaching (whether in preparation for an Ofsted inspection or not) is to ask an experienced colleague to observe you with a remit to comment upon:

- how you handle the context in which you are teaching (analyse choices made)
- what content you teach (clarity and appropriateness?)
- how you manage the process of teaching (flow of tasks)
- what are the learning outcomes at the end of your lesson (is the intended product achieved?)

Linking with other professional colleagues can also prove a valuable source of support and development. For example, all 16–19 teachers, but especially those in the arts and humanities, can benefit enormously from working closely with library staff. This can enhance your teaching by updating and broadening the range of resources you employ with your students. This might enable you to draw on colleagues' expertise to develop a range of interesting and stimulating material for students from different cultures and genres. This can then be used to supplement and extend recommended books and specified resources. Librarians may agree to provide a regularly updated press cuttings service for your classes if you provide clear guidelines and parameters on what would be helpful to support learning. This is even more important if your students could benefit from accessing high quality web sites, but you have limited access to check them. Librarians may be willing to offer advice on broadening book stocks and supporting e-learning. They may also build an archive of audio and video material to support your 16–19 teaching.

People within your school or college are often the most effective source of resources. However, in a subjects like Communication Studies or Media Studies, schools in particular often find such disciplines staffed by non-specialist English or Sociology teachers. This need not always be a disadvantage, provided opportunities for professional development are prioritised within the institution to support the effective teaching of such subjects. Teachers of these subjects should be encouraged to visit practitioners with their students, or to invite practitioners in to brief their students and to contribute to the assessment of project work.

For many school-based 16–19 teachers, the bulk of their responsibilities lie with the 11–16 environment. For them, it is understandably easy to lose touch with the demands of new knowledge and new approaches to teaching appropriate to the post-16 phase. Teachers might feel out-of-date and insecure in their limited 16–19 teaching. As a consequence it is possible that the teaching could be somewhat under-prepared, somewhat lacklustre and fail to engage increasingly passive students. It is a salutary reminder for developing effective 16–19 teaching skills that effectiveness can be given a pretty wide definition. In the 16–19 classroom, teacher artistry ((Hay McBer 2000) is important: know your subject, know your students and guide learning with deft control. The last comes with teacher perception in the classroom, teacher intuition, and a creative impulse. Working with colleagues to develop positive inter-relationships with students is a valuable start to effective 16–19 teaching.

CASE STUDY: HOW CAN A CAREER BE FORGED IN 16–19 TEACHING?

Although I did an 11–18 secondary PGCE course, I was interested in teaching the 16–19 age range. This was partly due to a curious notion of status I attached to having a Masters degree (in Victorian Studies) and wanting to use it, partly because of the kind of teaching style I favoured, and partly an antipathy to some of the 11–16 school discipline strategies I felt compromised by at the time. I attempted to use the opportunities to specialise in 16–19. For example, I elected to read up on 16–19 issues for some professional studies assessments (those were the days!). I do recall observing a very limited amount of 16–19 teaching during my time on teaching practice at a 13–18 comprehensive, but not being offered the chance to teach any.

However, happenstance had it that my professional tutor was the Professor/Head of department. Mentioning my interest in 16–19, he simply picked up the phone and got me an interview with the Head of department in the local FE college. Before I knew it, I was observing, and then being paid casually to teach part-time at the college before my PGCE was even finished. However, this was not A level teaching. These were the heady days of the Youth Training Scheme, and my role was with some very challenging students, school-failures all, who were doing a multi-skills course as a bridge between compulsory schooling and sheltered employment or the dole. I am not sure PGCE had prepared me for that. My point is an important one though. Twenty years ago, 16–19 education felt somewhat peripheral to a teacher's professional development. It was not at the centre of initial teacher education, and so it needed a pro-active approach to get a foot on to a relevant career ladder. Have things changed that much?

Starting off in a full-time post as an NQT did little to strengthen my position as an aspiring 16–19 teacher. Gaining a one-term temporary contract in an 11–18 comprehensive offered no sustained 16–19 classroom practice. I do remember my Head of Department kindly topping up my timetable with one hour per week of one-on-one teaching with a student who had changed courses and needed to catch up by studying *A Midsummer Night's Dream* for A level. However, this was hardly representative of the kind of skills I would need to develop in the 16–19 classroom.

However, jumping out of school and into a 'full-timetable' paid part-time FE teaching role after a term did expose me to a broad range of pre-vocational groups (more YTS, pre-YTS and some O level). Gaining a full-time post in another FE college gave me experience of servicing technician and craft teaching for other departments, and eventually GCSE and A level teaching.

The next big jump was back into a secondary school to a post managing and developing vocational and non-A level provision. This opened up CPVE, BTEC National and GNVQ, as well as an opportunity to introduce new academic subjects into a school sixth form. This evolved to include some mentoring of ITT placements, especially those trainees encountering 16–19 teaching for the first time. Undertaking a part-time Masters in Education by distance learning led to a doctorate focusing on learning to teach post-16, and a post in HE.

STARTING 16–19 TEACHING NOW

There are just as many issues facing the teachers today wishing to specialise in the 16–19 phase, or who wish to develop their career as credible 16–19 teachers. For example, the 2002 Green Paper opened up the space for potential synergies between school and FE teaching, which have until recently been mutually exclusive closed shops. How is a new teacher to interpret and respond to such opportunities? This question is particularly important, as the 16–19 phase looks increasingly like becoming part of a newly conceptualised 14–19 phase. Will A levels get taught like GCSEs, in which active teacher intervention complements some spoon-feeding? Or will GCSEs get taught like some A levels, aimed directly at high fliers. In addition, universities are becoming increasingly vociferous about how post-16 students have been taught and what skills and content they should have been taught. What impact will this have on the kind of teaching skills that 16–19 teachers in the future will need?

So what opportunities can teachers take up to support their career development as a 16–19 specialist, or as a credible 16–19 teacher? Serving as an AS or A level examiner, or an AS/A level coursework or AVCE portfolio moderator is both useful and important. Such roles can provide a really valuable insight into assessment processes which can bear fruit in an individual's own teaching. This need not be limited to the summer bout of script marking but can include specific tasks like question-setting and can develop into lead examining or Chief Examiner roles. The role of the visiting oral assessor also exists in a number of disciplines, and can provide invaluable staff development. Opportunities exist for 'repeat' post-16 GCSE examiners too. It is worth contacting the Awarding Bodies to register an interest after a few years of successful 16–19 teaching experience, particularly for those offering the specification you teach.

Subject associations are also important sources of support for the teacher interested in developing and updating their 16–19 teaching. Not only do they publish newsletters, which can include articles on 16–19 teaching, they also provide useful networks of colleagues through websites and electronic discussions. Local or regional networks for 'Heads of Sixth', post-16 tutors, 16–19 subject leaders or those with responsibility for HE entry can also provide valuable support and an opportunity to share ideas across very different institutional contexts. Do not neglect the possible benefits to be gained from serving as a school or college governor, particularly if you are able to take on a specific responsibility for 16–19 teaching and learning.

Of course the opportunity exists for teachers to extend their qualifications in a professionally orientated way through part-time advanced study at their local university or through distance learning. This could be through short courses, or a longer period of study accredited to Certificate, Diploma, Masters or Doctorate level. Relevant options can include:

- subject-knowledge enrichment suitable for enhancing 16–19 teaching
- management skills aimed at taking responsibility for leadership of a subject or course post-16
- engagement at postgraduate level with curriculum, learning or assessment theories relevant to 16–19 as part of a higher degree.

Forging informal and formal links with a local university, or a Higher Education institution to whom you regularly send students can also be productive. This can lead to the development of Compacts, which can enhance the opportunities for your students to progress on to study at an undergraduate level. It is also likely to lead to offers of talks to your students from HE staff, and to attendance at HE fairs and open days. A link is also valuable at results time in August, when some of your students may benefit from an established relationship with a university. The professional development opportunities for 16–19 specialists are many and varied.

If you find yourself working in a school or college providing 16–19 education for feeder 11–16 schools, it is also important to engage in and extend links by providing taster sessions, 'expert' teacher input and 16–19 roadshows. Authorative and knowledgeable 16–19 specialists play an important role in opening up access to educational opportunities for young adults.

It is likely that enhanced learning by 16–19 students requires sustained learning by teachers, and their schools or colleges. Is 16–19 teaching informed by a learning culture in your institution? Is research by teachers integral to provision? This can become even more important when the practicalities of many teachers' involvement in 16–19 teaching are taken into account. Secondary school teachers, or part-time college teachers, may have only a few hours 16–19 teaching per week. They may feel insecure about their subject knowledge, out-of-date in terms of assessment requirements and lacklustre in their approach to teaching strategies, especially if initially confronted with passive groups of learners. As individual teachers, and as members of departments, it is crucial they do retain a professional involvement in and enthusiasm for their limited 16–19 teaching.

It is not an appropriate response for 16–19 teachers to become hidebound to a regime of over-assessment and league tables. Rather, they should seek to develop the most effective teaching skills, which they can innovate within the current system. Successful schools and colleges need structured debate among teachers about 16–19 curriculum and teaching methods. Transparency about the mutual benefits of collaborative learning amongst 16–19 teachers is crucial.

HEADLINES

- If training in effective 16–19 teaching has been inadequate, it is important to work with a mentor and departmental colleagues to develop relevant skills.

10 Conclusion

Effective 16–19 teaching takes as much careful planning, alert classroom organisation and diligent assessment practices as any other teaching. This is a challenge for teachers when training has been relatively limited, and professional dialogue about 16–19 teaching is hard to find. This book has attempted to make explicit the intuitive craft knowledge which is easy to overlook or misunderstand when embarking on 16–19 teaching for the first time.

If a group of Martian educationalists popped down to observe 16–19 teaching in schools and colleges, would they be excited or depressed by what they saw? Prior to Curriculum 2000, one of the few books devoted to 16–19 education which actually discussed teaching skills (Macfarlane 1993) described A level teaching as stultifying. He cited teachers defending didactic methods on the grounds of: overlarge classes; inadequate resources; insufficient time and overloaded syllabuses. All the evidence from teachers and academic pundits recently has suggested very similar concerns in 16–19, which result in a comparable expedient reluctance to explore more effective teaching skills. How can 16–19 teachers regain a sense of professional autonomy and develop their classroom approaches?

Training does not help much at the moment: the training of 16–19 teachers is in a mess. As I have argued, 16–19 teaching demands particular nuances of approach. The academic literature underlines the uniqueness of the 16–19 context, whether full-time

---

OBJECTIVE

Reading this chapter and engaging actively with the tasks will enable you to:

- articulate a case for the importance of effective 16–19 teaching.

A level or AVCE teaching, in school sixth form or in a college environment. This uniqueness can be characterised as: dissimilar curriculum content, assessment methods and teaching approaches to those found in compulsory schooling or college-based pure vocational training. The pressing training need for 16–19 teachers is to enable them to manage the content on A level and AVCE courses, so that teaching approaches can be freer, more creative and sufficiently differentiated to meet the needs of the far wider range of learners now in 16–19 classes.

The current arrangements do not, on their own, produce effective 16–19 teaching. Initial training for those teachers working in 16–19 is usually split between 11–18 secondary PGCE (the norm for secondary and sixth-form college teachers) and a limited amount of full-time FE teacher training. In-service provision is almost all aimed at college teachers. Both have to meet different sets of Standards.

Training to teach 16–19 within secondary teacher training suffers from a low priority. The Standards have limited direct relevance, and mentor support is often targeted at competence in the 11–16 classroom. With increasing pressures on schools, access to sixth-form teaching is becoming more limited, and a number of 11–18 training courses are being redesignated 11–16. Schools rely on experienced 16–19 teachers for their improving results, but where are the next generation of passionate 16–19 teachers to come from?

FE teacher training is under critical scrutiny, and the absence of specialist mentor support is unhelpful preparation for A level teaching. As the two systems inch closer together, there is a vital need for some joined-up thinking in teacher training. Developments in the 14–19 curriculum may be the catalyst for this.

Of course trainee teachers will want to know how to make their 16–19 teaching effective enough to meet the Standards, and this book is a prompt for how those connections might be made. But 16–19 teaching in schools and colleges is far too complex to allow a direct simplistic relationship between teaching ideas and Standards. The critical link to effective 16–19 teaching is to open up dialogue with more experienced colleagues, and open up the 16–19 classroom door.

Effective 16–19 teaching skills depend to a large extent on generic approaches of support and challenge for all learners, which can be transferred across subject boundaries, according to context. The support comes from positive, active listening skills, and sets up a respectful relationship in which students feel they can make independent progress. The challenge must be introduced proportionately and realistically. Challenge too early, without trust established, and a student might withdraw. Too little challenge, and progress is unlikely to occur. There are clearly different emphases in different subjects, and indeed on different courses. But the similarities across disciplines outweigh the subject-specific particularities. Crucially, this is not to argue that generic approaches are applicable from 11–16 or established adult education approaches. The emphases needed in 16–19 are unique, and teachers need to plan and perform accordingly, taking best practice from other sectors as appropriate. But effectiveness in 16–19 teaching will uniformly draw on:

- confident presentation and mediation of relevant subject knowledge
- support for all learners building gradually to appropriate, individualised challenges
- well organised activities which build on previous learning and stimulate interest and engagement
- regular assessment feedback offering clear guidance and targets on progress
- warm, open dialogue with students.

Final Task

Get a group of experienced and inexperienced 16–19 teachers together in a department meeting. Brainstorm a series of (no more than ten) bullet points to describe factors which make for effective A level or AVCE teaching. Try to pool similar ideas and group them under headings. Now compare these to what Hay McBer have said about generic teaching skills, and what Ofsted has said about 16–19 teaching in your subject. Are there more similarities than differences? Do the generic points begin to merge with the subject-specific points?

Copy these ten bullet points to your 16–19 teaching colleagues in other departments, and await their versions. How close are your ten to their ten? It may be that there are three or four subject-specific points that are prioritised for each department, but after that more generally applicable ideas are likely to come through.

References

Andrews, R. (2001) *Teaching and Learning English*, London: Continuum.

Armitage, A., Bryant, R., Dunnill, R., Hayes, D., Hudson, A., Kent, J., Lawes, S. and Renwick, M. (2003) *Teaching and Training in Post-Compulsory Education* (2nd edn), Buckingham: Open University Press.

Arthur, J., Davison, J. and Moss, J. (1997) *Subject Mentoring in the Secondary School*, London: Routledge.

Bloomer, M. (1997) *Curriculum Making in Post-16 Education*, London: Routledge.

Bramald, R., Hardman, F. and Leat, D. (1995) 'Initial teacher trainees and their views of teaching and learning', *Teaching and Teacher Education*, 11 (1): 23–32.

Brown, C. (2001) 'Gender differences in subject choice', *Educational Studies*, 27 (2): 173–186.

Butcher, J. (1996) 'Alleviating tension at 16–19', *Forum for Comprehensive Education*, 38 (2): 41–49.

Butcher, J. (1998) 'The conundrum of GNVQ: a case study of the training needs of school-based GNVQ teachers', *Journal of Vocational Education and Training*, 50 (1): 569–583.

Butcher, J. (2000) 'Mentoring in professional development: the English and Welsh experience', in Moon, B., Butcher, J. and Bird, E. (eds) *Leading Professional Development in Education*, London: RoutledgeFalmer.

Butcher, J. (2002) 'A case for mentor challenge? The problem of learning to teach post-16', *Mentoring and Tutoring*, 10 (3): 197–220.

Butcher, J. (2003a) 'Sink or swim: learning to teach post-16 on an 11–18 PGCE', *Teacher Development*, 7 (1).

Butcher, J. (2003b) 'Exploring difficulties in learning to teach English post-16', *The Curriculum Journal*, 14 (2): 233–252.

Canning, R. (1999) 'Post-16 education in Scotland: credentialism and inequality', *Journal of Vocational Education and Training*, 51 (2).

Capewell, I. and Norman, E. (2003) 'The Sustainable Design Award: supporting 16-plus students in addressing sustainable design issues', *The Journal of Design and Technology Education*, 8 (2): 82–90.

Chitty, C. (ed.) (1991) *Post-16 Education*, London: Kogan Page.

Constable, A. (1999) 'A walk in Memphis – post-16 introductory project for design', *The Journal of Design and Technology Education*, 4 (2): 166–168.

Dart, L. and Drake, P. (1993) 'School-based training: a conservative practice?', *Journal of Education for Teaching*, 19 (2): 175–189.

Dart, L. and Drake, P. (1996) 'Subject perspectives in mentoring', in McIntyre, D. and Hagger, H. (eds) *Mentors in Schools*, London: David Fulton.

Davies, C. (1993) 'Ideologies of the subject and the professional training of English teachers' (thesis D.Phil.), University of Oxford.

Davies, C. (1997) 'Problems about achievement of shared understandings', in McIntyre, D. (ed.) *Teacher Education Research in a New Context*, London: Paul Chapman.

Daw, P. (1996) 'Achieving high grades at A Level English Literature: an investigation into factors that contribute to schools' successes', *English in Education*, 30 (3): 15–26.

Dearing, R. (1996) *Review of Qualifications for 16–19 Year Olds*, London: SCAA.

DfEE (1996a) 'Qualifying for success: post-16 curriculum reform', letter to schools, DfEE.

DfEE (1999b) *Learning to Succeed: A New Framework for post-16 Learning*, London: The Stationery Office.

DfEE (1999) *The Induction Period for Newly Qualified Teachers*, Circular 5/99, London: DfEE.

DfEE (2000) *Qualifying for Success: Changes to Post-16 Qualifications*, London: DfEE.

DfES (2002a) *Success for All: Reforming Further Education and Training*, London: HMSO.

DfES (2002b) *14–19: Extending Opportunities, Raising Standards*, consultation document, London: HMSO.

DfES (2004) *The Interim Report of the Working Group on 14–19 Reform*, London: DfES.

Drake, P. and Dart, L. (1994) 'Mentors in English and Mathematics', in Reid, I. (ed.) *Teacher Education Reform: Current Research*, London: Paul Chapman.

Drake, P. and Dart, L. (1997) 'Different perceptions of 'teacher competence' – trainees and their mentors', in Hudson, A. and Lambert, D. (eds) *Exploring Futures in Initial Teacher Education*, London: Institute of Education, University of London.

Eggleston, J. (2000) 'Staying on at 16+: a hidden curriculum of tutoring', *Mentoring and Tutoring*, 8 (2): 127–136.

Elliott, B. and Calderhead, J. (1995) 'Mentoring for teacher development: possibilities and caveats', in Kerry, T. and Shelton, A. (eds) *Issues in Mentoring*, London: Routledge.

Eraut, M. (1997) 'Curriculum frameworks and assumptions in 14–19 education', *Research in Post-Compulsory Education*, 2 (3): 281–298.

Fawbert, F. (ed.) (2003) *Teaching in Post-Compulsory Education*, London: Continuum.

Finegold, D., Keep, E., Miliband, D., Raffe, D., Spours, K. and Young, M. (1990) *A British Baccalaureate: Ending the Division Between Education and Training*, London: Institute for Public Policy Research.

French, D. (2002) 'Examining some changes in mathematics post-16', in Haggarty, L. (ed.) *Aspects of Teaching Secondary Mathematics*, London: RoutledgeFalmer.

Fullan, M. (2001) *The New Meaning of Educational Change* (3rd edn), New York: Teachers College Press.

Goodwyn, A. (1997) *Developing English Teachers*, Buckingham: Open University Press.

Graham, P. (1997) 'Tensions in the mentor teacher–student relationships: creating productive sites for learning within a high school English teacher education programme', *Teaching and Teacher Education*, 13 (5): 513–527.

Haggarty, L. (1995) 'The use of content analysis to explore conversations between school teacher mentors and student teachers', *British Educational Research Journal*, 21 (2).

Haggarty, L. (ed.) (2002) *Aspects of Teaching Secondary Mathematics*, London: RoutledgeFalmer.

Hardman, F. and Leat, D. (1998) 'Images of post-16 English teaching', *Teaching and Teacher Education*, 14 (4): 359–370.

Hardman, F. and Williamson, J. (1998) 'The discourse of post-16 English teaching', *Educational Review*, 50 (1): 5–14.

Harkin, J. and Davis, P. (1996) 'The communication styles of teachers in post-compulsory education', *The Journal of Further and Higher Education*, 20 (1): 25–34.

Harkin, J. and Turner, G. (1997) 'Patterns of communication styles of teachers in English 16–19 Education', *Research in Post-Compulsory Education*, 2 (3): 261–280.

Harkin, J., Turner, G. and Dawn, T. (2001) *Teaching Young Adults*, London: RoutledgeFalmer.

Harland, J. (1991) 'Upper secondary education in England and Wales: an overview of curriculum pathways', in Chitty, C. (ed.) *Post-16 Education*, London: Kogan Page.

Hay McBer (2000) *Research into Teacher Effectiveness*, Norwich: HMSO.

Higham, J. (1996) *Breadth in the Post-16 Academic Curriculum*, Occasional Publication No. 2: University of Leeds School of Education.

Higham, J., Sharp, P., Machin, D. and Wilson, M. (2000) 'Academic progress in the 16–19 curriculum: some senior staff perceptions of current monitoring systems and operational procedures', *The Curriculum Journal*, 12 (1): 59–80.

Hodgson, A. and Spours, K. (eds) (1997) *Dearing and Beyond*, London: Kogan Page.

Hodgson, A. and Spours, K. (2003) *Beyond A Levels: Curriculum 2000 and the Reform of 14–19 Qualifications*, London: Kogan Page.

Hodkinson, P. (1998) Review Essay: 'Education 14–19: critical perspectives', *British Journal of Educational Studies*, 46 (4): 468–470.

Holt, M. (1978) *The Common Curriculum*, London: Routledge & Kegan Paul.

Jones, J. (1996) 'The NQT experience in post-16 geography: research findings', in Powell, A. (ed.) *Handbook of Post-16 Geography*, Sheffield: The Geographical Association.

Judge, H. (1984) *A Generation of Schooling*, Oxford: Oxford University Press.

Kershaw, N. (1994) *An Unfinished Jigsaw: The 16+ Curriculum in the 1990s*, Bristol: The Staff College.

Knowles, M. (1984) *Andragogy in Action*, San Francisco: Jossey-Bass.

Lawton, D. (1992) *Education and Politics in the 1990s*, London: Falmer.

Le Versha, L. and Nicholls, G. (eds) (2003) *Teaching at Post-16*, London: Kogan Page.

Lucas, N. (1997) 'The applied route at age 14 and beyond: implications for initial teacher education', in Hudson, A. and Lambert, D. (eds) *Exploring Futures in Initial Teacher Education*, London: Institute of Education, University of London.

Macfarlane, D. (1993) *Education 16–19 in Transition*, London: Routledge.

McNally, P. and Martin, S. (1998) 'Support and challenge in learning to teach: the role of the mentor', *Asia-Pacific Journal of Teacher Education*, 26 (1).

Marland, M. (2003) 'The transition from school to university: who prepares whom, when and how?', *Arts and Humanities in Higher Education*, 2 (2): 201–211.

Molyneux-Hodgson, S. and Sutherland, R. (2002) 'Mathematics for post-16 vocational courses', in Haggarty, L. (ed.) *Aspects of Teaching Secondary Mathematics*, London: RoutledgeFalmer.

Naish, M. (1996) 'Curriculum development in A level courses', in Powell, A. (ed.) *Handbook of Post-16 Geography*, Sheffield: The Geographical Association.

National Commission on Education (1995) *Learning to Succeed After 16*, London: National Commission on Education.

Office for Standards in Education (Ofsted) (2001a) *Good Teaching, Effective Departments*, London: Ofsted.

Office for Standards in Education (Ofsted) (2001b) *Inspecting post-16: Art and Design*, London: Ofsted.

Office for Standards in Education (Ofsted) (2001c) *Inspecting post-16: Business Education*, London: Ofsted.

Office for Standards in Education (Ofsted) (2001d) *Inspecting Careers Education and Guidance*, London: Ofsted.

Office for Standards in Education (Ofsted) (2001e) *Inspecting post-16: Design and Technology*, London: Ofsted.

Office for Standards in Education (Ofsted) (2001f) *Inspecting post-16: Drama and Theatre Studies*, London: Ofsted.

Office for Standards in Education (Ofsted) (2001g) *Inspecting post-16: English*, London: Ofsted.

Office for Standards in Education (Ofsted) (2001h) *Inspecting post-16: Geography*, London: Ofsted.

Office for Standards in Education (Ofsted) (2001i) *Inspecting post-16: Government and Politics*, London: Ofsted.

Office for Standards in Education (Ofsted) (2001j) *Inspecting post-16: History*, London: Ofsted.

Office for Standards in Education (Ofsted) (2001k) *Inspecting post-16: Mathematics*, London: Ofsted.

Office for Standards in Education (Ofsted) (2001l) *Inspecting post-16: Media Education*, London: Ofsted.

Office for Standards in Education (Ofsted) (2001m) *Inspecting post-16: Modern Foreign Languages*, London: Ofsted.

Office for Standards in Education (Ofsted) (2001n) *Inspecting post-16: Music*, London: Ofsted.

Office for Standards in Education (Ofsted) (2001o) *Inspecting post-16: Physical Education*, London: Ofsted.

Office for Standards in Education (Ofsted) (2001p) *Inspecting post-16: Science*, London: Ofsted.

Office for Standards in Education (Ofsted) (2001q) *Inspecting post-16: Sociology*, London: Ofsted.

Office for Standards in Education (Ofsted) (2001r) *Inspecting School Sixth Forms*, London: Ofsted.

Office for Standards in Education (Ofsted) (2002a) *Inspecting post-16: Dance*, London: Ofsted.

Office for Standards in Education (Ofsted) (2002b) *Inspecting post-16: Psychology*, London: Ofsted.

Office for Standards in Education (Ofsted) (2003) *The Initial Training of Further Education Teachers*, London: Ofsted.

Office for Standards in Education (Ofsted) (2004a) *Developing New Vocational Pathways: Final Report on the Introduction of New GCSEs*, London: Ofsted.

Office for Standards in Education (Ofsted) (2004b) *Vocational A Levels: The First Two Years*, London: Ofsted.

Payne, J. (2003) 'The impact of part-time jobs in Years 12 and 13 on qualification achievement', *British Educational Research Journal*, 29 (4): 599–611.

Phillips, G. and Pound, T. (2003) (eds) *The Baccalaureate*, London: Kogan Page.

Polat, F., Kalambouza, A., Boyle, W. and Nelson, N. (2001) *Post-16 Transitions of Pupils with Special Educational Needs*, Nottingham: HMSO.

Pound, T. (1998) 'Forty years on: the issue of breadth in the post-16 curriculum', *Oxford Review of Education*, 24 (2): 167–180.

Powell, A. (ed.) (1996) *Handbook of Post-16 Geography*, Sheffield: The Geographical Association.

Pring, R. (1995) *Closing the Gap: Liberal Education and Vocational Preparation*, London: Hodder & Stoughton.

Qualifications and Curriculum Authority (QCA) (1998) 'The future of post-16 qualifications', press release, QCA.

Qualifications and Curriculum Authority (QCA) (1999) *Curriculum Guidance for 2000*, London: QCA.

Rainbow, B. (1993) 'Modular A and AS levels: the Wessex Project', in Richardson, W., Woolhouse, J., and Finegold, D. (eds) *The Reform of Post-16 Education and Training in England and Wales*, Harlow: Longman.

Richardson, W. (1993) 'The 16–19 education and training debate: deciding factors in the British public policy process', in Richardson, W., Woolhouse, J. and Finegold, D. (eds) *The Reform of Post-16 Education in England and Wales*, Harlow: Longman.

SCAA (1994a) 'A/AS Subject Cores: Briefing note', London: SCAA.

SCAA (1994b) 'Code of Practice for GCE A and AS Examinations', London: SCAA.

SCAA (1996) 'Draft Principles for A/AS Examinations', London: SCAA.

Sharp, P. (1997) *The Development of the Vocational Curriculum for 16–19 Year Olds in Colleges and Schools, 1979–1995*, Occasional Publication No. 5: University of Leeds School of Education.

Stanton, G. and Richardson, W. (1997) (eds) *Qualifications for the Future*, London: Further Education Development Agency.

Teacher Training Agency (TTA) (2002) *Qualifying to Teach: Professional Standards for Qualified Teacher Status and Requirements for Initial Teacher Training*, London: TTA.

Teacher Training Agency (TTA) (2003) *Career Entry and Development Profile*, London: TTA.

Turton, D. (1996) 'Teaching A level courses', in Powell, A. (ed.) *Handbook of Post-16 Geography*, Sheffield: The Geographical Association.

UCAS (2000) *Changes to Post-16 Qualifications*, Cheltenham: UCAS.

Watson, J., McEwen, A. and Dawson, S. (1994) 'Sixth-form A Level students' perception of the difficulty, intellectual freedom, social benefit and interest of Science and Arts subjects', *Research in Science and Technological Education*, 12 (1): 43–51.

Watts, A. and Young, M. (1997) 'Models of student guidance in a changing 14–19 training system', in Hodgson, A. and Spours, K. (eds) *Dearing and Beyond*, London: Kogan Page.

Whitbread, N. (1991) 'The Education Reform Act: a missed opportunity for 16+', in Chitty, C. (ed.) *Post-16 Education*, London: Kogan Page.

Zanting, A. (2001) *Mining the Mentor's Mind*, Leiden: Leiden University.

Index

eBooks

eBooks - at www.eBookstore.tandf.co.uk

A library at your fingertips!

eBooks are electronic versions of print books. You can store them onto your PC/laptop or browse them online.

They have advantages for anyone needing rapid access to a wide variety of published, copyright information.

eBooks can help your research by enabling you to bookmark chapters, annotate and use instant searches to find specific words or phrases. Several eBook files would fit on even a small laptop or PDA.

NEW: Save money by eSubscribing: cheap, online acess to any eBook for as long as you need it.

Annual subscription packages

We now offer special low cost bulk subscriptions to packages of eBooks in certain subject areas. These are available to libraries or to individuals.

For more information please contact webmaster.ebooks@tandf.co.uk

We're continually developing the eBook concept, so keep up to date by visiting the website.

www.eBookstore.tandf.co.uk